DUNES REVIEW

EDITORIAL BOARD

Thank you to this issue's Patrons:
Bronwyn Jones
Anne-Marie Oomen
Joan Richmond
Phillip Sterling
In Memory of John Pahl

COVER IMAGE: "Gravity" by Catherine Jacobi, 2025

3 children's life preservers from 1955, rocks, string

DUNES REVIEW

Volume 29 Issue 2
Fall/Winter 2025

CONTENTS

F = Fiction

CNF = Creative NonFiction

Land Acknowledgement

Dunes Review is published on the traditional lands of the Grand Traverse
Band of Ottawa and Chippewa Indians. It is important to understand
the long-standing history that has brought us to reside on the land, and
to seek to understand our place within that history. We give honor to the
Anishinaabe people for their continual contributions to the land and society.

Cover Artist's Statement

"Gravity" captures the emotional weight of childhood portrayed by three
life vests. Each incident, once small and unnoticed, gradually accumulates,
building in intensity until the weight becomes overwhelming. The tension
in the forms reflects the emotional burden they carry, each pull a reminder
of the lasting impact of their experiences. The artwork is meant to convey a
profound sense of struggle, vulnerability, and the quiet strength needed to
endure.

—Catherine Jacobi

Editors' Notes

Dear Readers, as I write this, my digital and postal mail boxes are filled with year-end donation appeals from nonprofit organizations--those entities whose work is crucial to a compassionate, expressive, healthy--indeed, fed!--society. Your reading this means that you, too, support the arts as a Michigan Writers member or as a writer. You likely know that the current political powers have cut federal public arts funding. Here in the state of Michigan, Republican House Speaker Matt Hall characterized arts funds as "an example of waste." Public pressure helped keep arts funding in the state budget. That story (from *Bridge* magazine) makes me mad that some leaders have such limited vision. But also it gives me hope that public commitment to the arts is deeply felt enough to forestall at least one small-minded decision. And I am more grateful than ever to the many people who keep this journal and other arts organizations going. Thank you for your continued support. I hope you enjoy this collection of work.

—Teresa Scollon

"I wonder how all this will turn out," Fleda Brown starts us off, setting the tone for this issue. "As if turning out were a thing." And that pretty much sums up a lot of my feelings about 2025, which sure has been A Year. I do wonder; we all do. How will this all turn out? All things change, certainly, whether thanks to our own volition or the inevitability of avalanches or other seismic shifts. The natural order of things demands disorder, assessment, adaptation, reorder.

I believe poets—and I'm using the term loosely here to encompass all creative writers, whether their lines are in verse or not—feel those seismic shifts particularly deeply. As such, we're compelled to express ourselves within the framework of them, to push against the shifts with language, to use words on a page to grapple with matters at hand. Does it help? I have to believe it does. It helps those who are writing—helping us make an iota of sense of the world and its chaos—and it helps those who read and listen, reminding us of our connectedness, our shared humanity in the face of both beauty and trouble.

"I don't / have the right color to write / about this," says Basil Payne. Rarely do we have quite the perfect pen, or voice, or words. But still, we essay. We try.

—Jennifer Yeatts

Fleda Brown
WEATHER

I wonder how this will turn out, as if turning out were a thing.
I lived in the century of decline, of collapse, of appearances.

Do people on their deathbed wonder how things will turn out?
No, they are too busy dying, which is a thing. It has stages

and then is over. I don't know what stage this living is in, now.
Living is clutching its roots, trying to gather nutrients from

the soil. Others are helping, leaching their nutrients over.
If you are living in a different time, when this has turned out

some unimaginable way, imagine our suffering, so unlike
yours, closer to the planet's end, having somehow gotten

through all those catastrophes, but they've kept coming,
like wind and rain. It's weather, that's what it is. There's

a plastic bucket left, and a tent, and a neighbor is going to
share her soup made out of scraps, to get you by once again.

Shuly Xóchitl Cawood
REFRIGERATOR, 2025
after Thomas Lux

My husband wanted a new one, didn't want to worry about
the other breaking down, which it was starting to, having trouble
keeping everything as cold as we wanted. I didn't mind

fiddling, pushing up the temperature tab on the inside
and asking the appliance to work a little harder. *You can do this*,
I wanted to say but never did, maybe because for a while now

I've been telling myself that, and sometimes I don't think
I can, not really, or at least not well. My husband
went ahead and got a new one—rated well by Consumer Reports

and one that would fit in the space carved out below
our hard-to-reach cabinets that hold paper plates and plastic cups
for those parties we never have anymore. Cocktail napkins

in bright colors, and a bottle of wine that perhaps we are making
more valuable by keeping it for years shoved
in the back. We've never been wine drinkers. My husband

likes a good IPA and I would probably love a sweet and fruity
cocktail but have a body that does not tolerate drinks. So I sip
water, so much water I could be an ocean. I would know

exactly how to crash against a shore. My husband is happy
with this new appliance: its two-drawer freezer which makes
our cold adobe chicken dinners, my sweet potato chili, and all those

nuts we buy in bulk so much easier to find. I don't think about
our old refrigerator much, or ask myself where it might be now.
I find that question impossible to answer, and I don't want

to cry about what is gone for good. That old appliance stayed
longer in my life than some people do. In its freezer, once, I left a whole
bag of frozen berries that melted and leaked into the white plastic

liner of the drawer. That bag thawed and then refroze, a thing we all do:
regret but don't admit, move on and pretend none of it ever happened,
tell ourselves we can walk away without a single stain.

Ellen Lord
SUMMER OF 2025: ARE WE STARDUST?
*—Written after Trump bombed Iran
listening to Joni Mitchell sing "Woodstock"*

Are we destined for darkness—
caught in the devil's bargain?

Galaxies of starglow fade
as flares of 'bunker-buster bombs'
penetrate the night sky.
He calls it 'Operation Midnight Hammer'!?
like the title of an Epstein sex tape—
and somewhere, a potentate
says drones are butterflies.

And who is hungry for the music
of freedom?
Does Gaza's child of God
want to join a rock 'n' roll band
as she holds her empty bowl
into a raging sky?
Who—
is going to set her soul free?

Today I'm grappling with faith, but I want
to believe Mitchell when she sings—
Life is for learning.
So, please, walk beside me.
I have come here to find a friend—
to help us, help us—
get back to the garden.

How we yearn for light. To be golden.
Such a quiet thing.

Jan Worth
A DAY WITH A ROETHKE SCHOLAR
IN TROUBLED TIMES

for William Barillas

In the bedroom where my friend slept last night
I hung a Roethke poem: The Waking,
of course. It is right there, the relief
of its twining lines, its circular bravery:
"I feel my fate in what I cannot fear,"
the child of flowers writes.

So it is no accident that all day
since breakfast
we have been talking
about poetry, and then
wandering out after several hours
into the clean sanctuary air
of a museum we both have loved
for years.

The Roethke scholar says
he is feeling exceptionally weepy
these days, and I say the same.
We both are on medicines
designed to help, but
the losses cannot be denied
even in these inviting rooms.

At a Sisley landscape*, my eyes and ardor follow
a path toward a person in the scene. A man
stands in a bend of sunlight, surrounded

by autumn shadow. I'm already imagining
the poem I might write about it, lines for how
I want to walk toward that carpet of light.

Late afternoon back home,
my husband joins us, completing
a trio of history and affection.
We eat lamb chops, asparagus,
and little potatoes doused with butter
at a sturdy table with a blue cloth,
And then we go out to
lawn chairs and fieldstones,
as if the house can't contain us,
talk spilling out, espresso
of words and cherished memories.

In the green shade of this, my own modest palette,
a stalwart oak bends over us.
I show the Roethke scholar my
trillium, mayapple, blooming bloodroot
and yellow archangel

and I am drinking small quaffs of beaujolais,
the sound of that word a pleasure in my mouth
even before the wine and
I am in love despite the approaching dark
with our voices and the breathing silences
between them, the soft ground
of our words.

* "Edge of a Forest in Autumn"
https://collections.flintarts.org/objects/111/

David B. Guenther
THE ANCHOR

In Cedarville, Michigan, a Saturday morning in May meant going fishing. Heuck and I got up early, stepped down the woodchip path from the Big Cottage on Big LaSalle Island into the boat he called the Grady White, pushed off from the wood-piling dock, and after Heuck had gotten the engine started, motored up the channel toward the Hessel bass spot. The light was still grey, the temperature in the low 50s; the water was dead calm under an overcast sky; and a mist hung over the channel, obscuring the cedar treeline and scattered cottages along the shore. The boat gained speed and leveled off. Past Islington Point the shoreline fell away, and in Islington Bay, there was only the water, the mist, and us in the boat in the middle of it.

We would fish with plastic worms. They weren't exactly plastic; they were kind of gummy, slightly tacky to the touch — some of them apparently scented — and the fish in any event didn't seem to know the difference. I'd bought them at a new sporting goods store in Gaylord on the way up from Ann Arbor. In the past we would have gone to the Cedarville Pantry, which had since been bought by some kind of corporate conglomerate and rebranded as the E-Z Mart, for live chubs, fishing them out of the tank in the back with a small net, or possibly nightcrawlers in black soil in little white styrofoam containers. With the chubs, we would have used bobbers, hooking the chubs through the upper lip and casting them out with three or four feet of line below and waiting for a bass or a pike to strike and pull the bobber under. You had to give the pike some time to commit. They often seemed to carry the chub loosely in their mouths for eight or ten seconds, and if you reacted too soon, they would just let go, so you had to wait and watch the bobber pull this way and that underwater before you tried to set the hook. The smallmouth didn't wait. With the nightcrawlers, we'd attach a small sinker and cast. The trick was to figure out where the currents were, let your worm be carried along where the smallmouth might be waiting, and avoid snagging your hook in the reeds or on the rocky bottom.

Now, ever since Heuck had gotten Lyme disease, he'd developed an aversion to killing anything, no matter how

insignificant, even a chub or an earthworm, let alone a fish. A few
years before, he'd been bitten by a tick, on the back of his leg behind
the knee, and hadn't noticed—growing up, there had never been
ticks in Cedarville or anywhere else in Michigan, so he hadn't been
in the habit of checking—until his knee had become inflamed, and
a whole host of other debilitating, increasingly systemic symptoms
had gradually manifested, and after six months it had gotten so bad,
he'd been afraid he had ALS. The doctors, with some prodding, had
eventually determined it was Lyme disease. They'd pumped him full
of antibiotics for six months or a year, and he'd gradually, for the
most part, recovered. But the experience had left him, and the rest
of our small circle—friends for forty years, since college, all of us
now approaching sixty—with a new awareness of mortality. In the
past, we would have kept whatever fish we caught, and after gutting
and scaling them, fried them up for breakfast. The smallmouth were
always better eating than the pike, which could have a sour taste, plus
you had to watch out for all the little pike bones, and sometimes—we
all agreed—the pike seemed to give you strange dreams. But anything
we caught now, we'd throw back in.

In the smooth morning water we rounded the point, motored
up Snows Channel, past Dollar Island, the still-deserted golf course
to the right, and the big houses of the Les Cheneaux Club on the
wooded hill to the left, until we approached the narrow mouth of a
swampy little bay to our right, on the mainland side. Heuck eased
back on the throttle, then cut the engine. He clambered forward,
hefted the anchor, which was tied with a white nylon rope to a cleat
on the bow, and after we'd drifted far enough forward, where we'd
be able to cast into the narrow mouth, slowly lowered the anchor into
the water. The boat stopped moving. There was no wind. The anchor
held on the sandy bottom.

Heuck clambered back from the bow, sat back down in the
captain's seat, opened the tackle box on the deck and handed me a
gummy worm. It was time to bait up.

"I was trying to remember, when was the first time you came
up here, anyway?" he said, as I hooked my gummy worm.

"It must have been 1983 or '84," I said. I selected a small lead
sinker from a little round container in the tackle box, threaded the
loose line from my pole through the sinker's open end, and bit down
carefully on the sides to secure it a few feet up from the worm. "I
remember that time we came up with Gerry and those two women

from Boston—I'd already been here at least once, and that was in 1984, in the summer after we graduated—so it had to have been before that."

"1983 or '84—that's almost forty years ago," Heuck said. "A lot of water under the bridge."

"Yeah," I said, ticking mentally through marriages, divorces, kids born and raised and scattered across the globe, careers built, changed, ended, people retiring, some already dead. "A lot of water."

The Big Cottage, as it was called, had been built by Heuck's great-grandfather in something like 1906. When I first saw it, the interior had still been pretty spartan—the wood floors, walls and ceilings had been black with age and oxidation. A few years later Heuck had gotten married in Pittsburgh, and his wife hadn't liked the look of the place—it was old and dark and dingy, and it didn't matter if it had always looked that way— so after an extended family debate, she had prevailed, and the interior had been refinished. The floors and walls had been sanded, the ceilings painted white. There were new bathrooms with showers, a dishwasher and other new appliances, flower pots on the front steps, woodchips and solar lanterns along the paths in front. The whole cottage had been out of plumb, so the doorways and windows had been visibly crooked, which made the place drafty and cold, and eventually they'd had to have everything jacked up and replace the old cedar tree trunk pilings underneath with concrete cinder blocks. Heuck had counted the rings on one of the old pilings. There had been one hundred fifty, plus or minus. If the cottage had been built in 1906, that meant those trees had started growing in the 1750s. The old pilings were now out in the firewood lean-to in back. But with the doors and windows all squared up, the cottage now felt snug.

I stepped toward the stern of the boat, rod in hand, reel face open and index finger pressing my line against the pole, and released as I cast my gummy worm. At the Hessel bass spot, the idea had always been to cast into the outlet at the mouth of the little swampy bay, either near or far, depending which way the water was moving, and let your worm sink down to a place where the current would take it. When the current shifted, which it seemed to do unpredictably from time to time, the bass would often strike. The waters around Cedarville had been rising and falling for years and were now close to an all-time high, however, so the outlet was deeper, and the current, if any, was different, and you had to cast in different places. If you could cast to the right place, the bass still seemed to strike the same way, when the current shifted. Their habits hadn't changed, anyway. But now there were also new fish in the water. Recently, further back, in what used to be the marsh, Heuck had caught a largemouth bass. Growing up in Michigan, I'd never seen one.

After half an hour of nothing, Heuck said, "Let's move."

He pulled the anchor up, and we shifted to a couple other spots, the first one out in the open bay, along a low shoal that had been a narrow little island but was now submerged, where one summer we'd caught something like thirty-five smallmouth in an hour and a half; and then, after getting nothing there, to the point of Eagle Island in Duck Bay, where we drifted for a few minutes, casting along the stony shoreline and the edge of the reeds, but still getting nothing.

"Let's try Middle Entrance," Heuck said.

Heuck, I knew, was not patient when fishing. He often said that fish would strike the moment your worm or lure hit the water. I'd seen it once or twice. But Heuck had been fishing these waters his whole life, summers anyway, so I figured he probably knew better. Plus he was a better fisherman than I.

Middle Entrance—the open passage between Little Lasalle and Marquette islands out into Lake Huron, the big lake—was another regular fishing spot. We'd fish the rocky point off Little LaSalle in Muskie Bay, practically just across from Duck Bay. A long line of boulders and big rocks extended out from the point into the bay for maybe a hundred yards underwater, some just under the surface, at least when the water was high, with the current and the wind sometimes moving in different ways on the bay and Middle Entrance sides, which made it a good place for big pike and bass to hang out and see what turned up. It was a good spot for bobber fishing, if the fish were biting. It was also a good place to get snagged, especially if you were using a sinker or casting with a spinner. One year we'd even lost an anchor there in the rocks. It had gotten wedged in so tight, we hadn't been able to pull it back up, and we'd had to cut the yellow nylon rope and leave it.

I cast my gummy worm a few times back toward the island, along the line of submerged rocks. A breeze rose and fell from around the point, rippling the surface of the water. The mist thinned and dissipated. Wispy clouds overhead broke here and there, revealing a glimpse of blue sky, a flash of sun, the depths of the channel beneath us vanishing momentarily in the reflection, until the clouds shifted, the low grey sky covered everything, and we could see boulders underwater again. A loon call somewhere was swallowed up in the distance. Sometimes the whole world seemed to be in motion. Our small boat floated, bobbed, drifted in the midst of it.

It wasn't ten minutes before I got snagged. Sometimes, if you raised the rod and pulled on the line, exerting a gentle but continuous pressure, the snag would come loose. But this time I found the snag yielding without coming loose; whatever it was, it was heavy, but it was moving. Sometimes a big sluggish pike would feel like that, but I knew that was probably wishful thinking.

"Looks like I've got a tree branch or something," I said.

I had the tip of my rod raised high, rod bending, line tense, and was reeling it slowly in, when a long squiggly yellow shape came into view. My line was hooked into the side of it. I realized it was a yellow nylon rope. Heuck leaned over the gunwale, grabbed hold of the rope, and began to pull, arm over arm, and lo and behold, as one final heave revealed, at the end of it was an anchor. Heuck laid the dripping anchor on the boat deck and stared.

"I don't believe it," he said, examining the anchor markings and the way the line was knotted. "It's the same anchor we lost here like thirty years ago."

"No way," I said. "What are the odds?"

We fished for another half hour without catching anything and headed back to the cottage. In the early evening, a chill wind kicked up out of the north, and from the overcast sky, a light rain began to fall. I got tumblers from the kitchen cupboard and went to the drink cart in the living room and poured us both a Scotch from the open bottle, with a splash of water, as Heuck built a fire in the fireplace.

"That was a strange thing today, that business with the anchor," he said, sitting cross-legged in his socks on the brick hearth, crumpling up a sheet of newspaper and pushing it under the iron grate in the fireplace. "Thirty-some years later, we wind up in the exact same spot and pull it up on the end of a snag. The exact same anchor."

He struck a match and lit the newspaper. Flames flared up the cobblestone chimney, and the dry wood began to crackle.

"Like it's been waiting there," he continued, "holding us—like we've been tied to it somehow the whole time."

"Well, maybe we have been," I said, taking a sip of my Scotch.

Heuck had always been bound to that place, I thought; his whole life was intertwined with it. I wasn't so sure about my own. But maybe forty years was enough. Skies had clouded and cleared, waters risen and fallen, seasons come and gone, and generations passed, one after another, as the world had changed around us, and we ourselves had aged and changed within. But the lake had endured, and evidently the anchor, and the mortal cord of our friendship, stretching back into our youth, that bound us to it. Perhaps that was enough.

"How's your Scotch?" I said. "Did I put enough water in?"

"Perfect," Heuck said.

Outside, the light faded. The north wind gusted from across the channel. Later we'd put one of the old cedar pilings on the fire. The old cedar would burn all night.

Eve Bainbridge
AT GALATOIRE'S

You buried faith
in browned butter, greens,
champagne breaking on lemon and gin.

A gentleman pours
glass after glass of cool water.

We flood;
outside, the river collapses
into myth.

Your throat,
shattered with high laughter,
lilac with blood,
holds no future sounds.

Your hands,
faded moths,
wing over the age-slick floor.

Your eyes, now glass,
trace the climb of fleur-de-lis.
I watch, hand to cheek,
say nothing,
drink your shining by mistake.

Camille Newsom
HER NAME IS SEX

she's queen of the chore chart, gold
stars for active, black X for dead.

she's amusing like bowling. she's drawn
with chalk, with fingers on steamed glass,

with expos on whiteboard. she's school distraction.
she's spoken turbulence. she's the lie at the dinner table,

on the doctor's exam table, bareback on stallion,
already jumping. she's the only time being watched

enhances performance, opposite of parallel parking
or [insert anything you suck at]. she's a tool,

the one you're always looking for and can't find,
the right-sized-wrench, the DD battery,

the one you need to turn on
the light. she's slowdancing

with room for jesus. she's a proud sinner.
she's sugar and violence. she's texting and driving.

she's hazy and she'll admit it, frothing
at perishables, suckling, behaving like fluid.

she hates religion, obviously in on the big cosmic joke,
easily cast as the haunter and/or the haunted.

Diane Glancy
INTERCHANGE

Interstate and frontage road— the bowling alley and return rail for the ball. Mowed by the scrape-work of de Kooning. His method of removing paint. The interchange of elements. De Kooning must have been a bowler— his throw of motion. The shapes without transition. His table crowded with jars and cans and paint tubes. It was a slash of tires. A stab of paint. The disjunction of roads to Sisyphus Lanes. Beyond the blinking palm-tree on the counter where the bowling-shoes were handed out.

Ella Shively
PLUSH BREATHERS
after "Nature" by Mary Oliver

That first night, when I, the failed
homeotherm, bedded down
in the warm tangle of your sheets,
I heard the owls perform a mad duet,
voices rising and sliding against one another
until I could not be certain
if they were singing or screaming.
You scraped your teeth across my throat,
the pulse a running animal,
rabbit-fast and hot.

I showed you the figure
in my ecology textbook once,
the twisting simulation of hare and lynx,
born to whirl imperfect circles
one around the other like a growing
strand of DNA.

Outside your window
a rabbit screamed, and your hair
was feather-soft against my cheek.
Your hands were talons;
I only pretended not to see.

Basil Payne
A RUN THROUGH THE UNDERBRUSH

It's not like I was sad,
just cold. Some light touched me.

□

Years after, I still feel
her hand cupping my cheek
like she found water after
a season of drought—not
even a chance she'd risk
a drop—pinky trailing my
carotid. Soft of my neck
against soft of her hand.
Only callous on her pointer
from practice each morning
on her marimba piece long enough
that she would meld with
the lower rosewood bars—
tremendous, like a heart.
Fingers on my neck, she knew
that I knew that she knew that
I loved her more than I should have.

□

Her favorite three songs on my playlist
were from a movie I wouldn't have watched
with anyone else. Her pinky on my carotid.
Her thumb on my carotid. Pressure on
the cusp between comfort and hurt—
liminality of her grasp before she clenched.
She held me whenever the screen went dim.

□

Red lines almost
like the usually-invisible
ones connecting
constellations
at night. How
sweet and bright.
Cuts from Western Ninebark
up my calves. Blood — beaded
pretty like worn jasper —
downward drips.
I want to do this again;
I need this again.
If anyone asks,
I tripped. I'm clumsy
enough for them
to believe it.

If you anthropomorphize to suit your needs,
trees actually enjoy losing branches.
Less weight, less to lose,
less to hold onto.
Less for wind to grab and challenge the roots holding everything together.

Basil Payne
FOR A PURPOSE SO FAR UNMAPPED

Hurt is a location; assault is, too,
and it's all there now, topography:
mountain spine exposed to you,
bruises every other peak or so,
dark-gray-purple like honey locust
shadows in noonday sun and the
clouds tonight. They change
the same way bruises do—slow
to color, too fast and too late.
On my map, I'd mark a forest
here. Here, too. Douglas fir so
thick that you'd think the mountain's
made of trees. Boxelder Maple
along the rivers, dense enough
that the sounds of river, rain, and
leaf become all but separate.
Build soft mountains all around
my groves, but it's barren. I don't
have the right color ink to write
about this. Sun's giving up and
the bruises are only purpeling.
The map, for now, will stay
whatever color uncharted territory
should be. What I wish was uncharted.

Glen Young
LEAVING THE ENCAMPMENT

What we talk about when we talk about the Rainbow Motor Lodge
is more how the river tumbled through town beneath the bridge
near the public hot springs, the few fish feeding as we leaned over
the metal rail, or how those cartoon-dark clouds dropped nearly to
the rough ground at the edge of the Encampment, as black caddis
buzzed the air atop the currents, diving and dying in a show of grace
and light. What we don't talk about enough is her bruised lip, the red
lights strobing in the dark of the parking lot, or the dark weather
in his eyes when he's led away, hands cuffed, shirt sleeve torn. What we
don't talk about is the way she, damaged and darker, drew blood where
before it was thunder, lightning, the rain when summer ended at their un-
doing, or how Highway 130 arced us into the Medicine Bow range, home,
though what we talked about on the drive is rivers, maps, the garbled syntax
of other weather and the nest of what once passed for arms and legs in love.

Mollie Thomas
EVEN FLOWERS

I was at the Ace Hardware on Elm Street to put up a flyer and I couldn't find a tack. The flyer said, "Have you seen my bike?" I read online that it was better to ask a question, rather than make a statement, like "Lost bike." Plus, my bike wasn't "lost," it was stolen.

The rest of the flyer went on to describe the bike in detail. Silver Bianchi from the '80s. Teal handlebar tape. Red water bottle holder. Last known location: Corner of First and Waverly, 8 pm Saturday, September 29. I figured I didn't need to mention that it was outside the bar, lest people start blaming me.

I was standing under the fluorescent lights, searching the board for a couple spare tacks with no luck. I got in line to ask the cashier for some.

"Do you have any more tacks?" I asked when it was my turn.

"Tacks?" Her nametag said her name was Ashley.

"Yeah, tacks." I held up my poster. "For the board back there," I said, pointing.

She looked at her coworker, a 60-something year-old woman wearing a pale-yellow turtleneck under her red vest. "Do you know if we have tacks?"

"Hmm," the woman said. "I think if we did, they'd be in aisle six, by the art supplies."

"No, not to buy. I need them for that board," I said, turning and pointing again.

"Oh!" She said, surprised. "Oh, gosh. I don't know, honey. You want to just leave it with us, and we can put it up once there's room?"

I felt my eyes narrow. I didn't trust her. I didn't trust her in her turtleneck, or "Ashley" who seemed high school aged but here she was, on a weekday at 2 pm, here at Ace. I told them I'd find a spot.

I walked to the back and again scanned the board of community offerings: A kids theater production of Alice in Wonderland, a take-a-tab hotline for domestic violence, the annual chili cookoff at the library. Then I noticed a flyer for a garden tour. It was happening that coming weekend, which I thought seemed late for a garden tour. October. Wasn't everything in the garden dead? And weren't garden tours usually put on by some club, with multiple stops? This was a homemade flyer, for just one person's house. I took a photo with my phone. I stole a few tacks where people had oversecured their posters and squeezed mine in. Ashley and Turtleneck were watching me as I left, talking in hushed tones, sharing a bag of the free popcorn.

As I left the store, I called my friend Sammy. He didn't answer. I texted him the photo of the flyer. *Want to go to this with me?*

What is it? He responded, immediately.

It's a garden tour. Why didn't you answer my call?

I'm in class. He meant teaching, not taking. He taught art at the high school.

Do you want to go to the tour?

Sure.

❖ ❖ ❖ ❖ ❖

That Saturday, Sammy and I met for breakfast before heading over. When I showed up to the restaurant, he was already in a booth reading a book. He was wearing a faded black t-shirt with his high school band's name on it. I remember seeing their first show. It was at a rented Elks Hall, none of us being old enough to be in a bar late at night.

I slid in across from him, noticing the butcher paper on the table had been adorned with a Sammy original: an illustration of a bouquet—mums and black-eyed Susans, ferns and non-descript autumnal flowers. Underneath it said, "Good morning, Madisen." A pile of broken, naked crayons sat at the edge of the table.

"Wow," I said. "Thanks for the flowers."

Sammy shrugged. "Seemed appropriate, given where we're headed."

I wiggled out of my corduroy jacket. "Indeed," I said.

"Have you ever been to a garden tour?" Sammy asked.

I shook my head. "Never," I said. The waitress came by, and I ordered a coffee.

"So why are we going to this one?"

I thought about the question for a second before answering. "Did you look at the flyer?" I asked. "Someone made that. It's not, like, part of a bigger event. Just one person wants to show off their garden, to anyone who wants to see it."

"Right," said Sammy.

"I guess I want to meet that person," I said. "And see that garden." The waitress set down my coffee. "And you're coming with me in case the person turns out to be a murderer."

23

"So we can both get killed."

"Correct."

✽✽✽✽✽

Sammy and I walked from breakfast into The Hills. The Hills is the nicest neighborhood, where anyone who works at the college lives. It's only blocks away where from the students live, but it has a distinct vibe to it. Lots of bungalows. Lots of home security signs. I kept checking the flyer, reminding myself of the address: 114 North Lake Ave. 114 North Lake Ave. 114 North Lake Ave.

"Any leads on your bike?" Sammy asked.

"Nope." I told him. "One week already. I think it's probably gone forever."

Sammy was quiet then. I looked at the picture of the flyer again.

"Are you going to get a new one?" He asked, after I tucked my phone back into my pocket.

"Can't," I said. "No money." I said, then pointing to the sign, "oh look—North Lake Ave. This is where we turn." I looked down the street left then right, trying to figure out which way 114 would be.

Sammy turned to face me on the sidewalk. "I could loan you some."

"I think we turn this way," I said, guiding us left. Sammy followed me.

"You need a bike," Sammy continued.

I looked at him, cocking my head to the side. "I know," I said, then turned back toward the sidewalk. "But no."

"Why not?"

"Sammy," I said. "You don't need to take care of me."

"I'm not taking care of you, Madisen. Being a good friend isn't 'taking care of you.' It's just... it's just being a good friend!"

"Thank you, but I don't need your help."

He threw up his hands in the air. "Oh, come on," he said. "Yes, you do."

"What?" I said, incredulous.

"You need my help all the time. You're constantly calling me to come over and look at something at your house, or to go out to dinner, or come with you on random journeys like... like to see a garden tour!"

"That's not *helping* me, Sammy. That's just friendship."

"Exactly!" Sammy said and started walking away, then turned around. "But why do you get to pick and choose how I show up? It's all just up to you. I'm always here but only when you want me."

"I don't even know what you're upset about, honestly. Sorry I don't want to take money from you?"

"Forget it." He looked up from where he was standing. "What's the address again?"

"114 North Lake Avenue," I told him.

"There it is," he said, pointing across the street at a brick house.

There was a wood board hanging above the porch with 114 painted in yellow. The front door and trim were painted green. There were worn wicker chairs set up, a table between them with a big red candle sitting on a small tin plate. A brick walkway headed to the backyard, where there was a fence and an arched door. A small sign that said 'garden tour this way' was taped to the door. It was curling up at the edges, dimpled with rain drops. "I guess we go back there."

"Guess so," said Sammy, waiting for me to lead the way.

Opening the gate didn't immediately reveal anything. It looked like more of the front yard. When we rounded the corner, I caught my breath. The garden was beautiful. It took over the entire back yard. Flowers and trees, grasses and bushes. The yard was a rainbow of fall colors and textures; goldenrod and fuchsia, velvety blooms, feathering reeds. A woman was sitting at a small table, scribbling in a notebook.

I went to say something, but my mouth was dry and I coughed instead, then cleared my throat. She looked up.

"Oh hi! Hello!" the woman said, setting her notebook down. She stood up and came over to us. She had to be at least 80, her blue eyes shining through hooded lids. She held onto my forearm when she reached me, I wasn't sure if it was a welcoming touch or if she was steadying herself. "I'm so glad you made it."

"Yeah, thanks." I said, taking a few steps back. "I'm Madisen." I said, in case she thought I was someone else, someone she was expecting. "And this is Sammy."

She smiled at Sammy, then at me again. "Madisen." She said. "Sammy." Another beat. "Beautiful."

I shifted on my feet. Too much direct eye contact. "So, yeah," I said, "I saw your flyer at Ace Hardware."

"Oh, good, good," she said. "You're my first attendees!"

I had a feeling we might be her only attendees. I turned toward the yard. "This is really gorgeous."

"Oh yes, thank you." She said nodding. "It was my husband's. He died a couple weeks ago."

I felt the air in my lungs swell and opened my mouth to say something. Sorry, surely, is what I would have said. Sammy spoke before I could get my lips to move.

"I'm so sorry," Sammy said. It was the first time he had spoken. It seemed to startle her.

"I know." She said, smiling warmly at Sammy, like he was the one who needed comfort. "He was sick for a long time." She added and I noticed her eyes had filled with big heavy fat tears that were about to fall. She took a short breath in and let it back out, clapped her hands together, then wiped both her eyes at once. "So. I don't really know anything about gardening. I'll never be able to keep it going. Figured I should show it off," she shrugged her shoulders, "before it's gone."

She told us about her husband, about his years of teaching at the college, not retiring until just a few years before he died. They had been married for 22 years, second marriages for them both. She sold ad space for the newspaper but had retired a long time ago. She spent winters in Mexico by herself, not a fan of the cold Ohio weather. Listening to her speak about her life like that, it was the first time I enjoyed hearing about someone's marriage. It wasn't like the marriages I knew. Like my sister who had completely changed her whole personality when she got married, suddenly *super* into hunting and acting like living in the middle-of-nowhere, Oklahoma was exactly where she always wanted to be. Or my mom, who since my dad died a decade ago, has fallen apart at the seams and can't seem to get it together.

"And you two," she said, gesturing at us, "are you married?"

"Us? No." I smiled at Sammy, "no, I'm not his type."

"That's not true," Sammy said, frowning.

She smiled at us without showing her teeth. "Well," she said, blinking once. "Lots of time."

I wasn't sure what she meant by that and looked over at Sammy to get his read. He was pretending to look at the flowers, avoiding my eyes. "Ok, come on," she said, "let's start this tour." She slowly walked us around the garden – though, she didn't really know the names of any of the plants. No trivia to share. It was clear she respected the garden but didn't actually care enough to learn much about it. We stopped every couple of steps, agreed about how beautiful it all was. She asked if we wanted to take home a bouquet and had us follow her to the garage to grab the shears.

Sammy had to duck to walk through the glass-paned door. Inside was a Ford hatchback, a work bench with a clean surface, surrounded by tools hanging, outlined by marker on the cream-colored peg board. She opened drawers, moved gloves.

"Here we are," the woman said, holding up a pair of orange-handled shears. "You two take these and start cutting, I'll grab a couple of vases for you to take home."

Sammy and I were in the garden, tentatively cutting a few flowers. Neither of us knew how to make a bouquet and though she had told us to, it still felt a bit like stealing.

"Did you see that tool outline situation?" I said quietly, leaning into Sammy's shoulder so he could hear me.

"Yeah," he said, shifting his weight so I wasn't pressed against him.

"Her husband must have been a real pill," I added. But he wouldn't budge. Clearly, he was pissed. "What's wrong?" I asked.

"Nothing," he said, looking at me finally. His hazel eyes looked tired.

"Sammy," I said, laughing a little. "Come on. I'm sorry."

"For what?".

I didn't know exactly what to apologize for. He was made of gold and I was always too mean or too selfish, and honestly I often wondered why he kept hanging out with me other than the fact that we'd been hanging out for a decade. I looked at him then, he was sitting on the dirt on his knees looking at my face. "It's okay, Madisen," he finally said. "It's fine."

"Here you go," the woman said, coming out with a vase in each hand. She gave one to me and one to Sammy. "Don't be timid, now. Make a big, beautiful bouquet." She shuffled over to her chair, where we had first found her. "I'm just going to sit over here, rest a bit."

Sammy and I thanked her and got back to work cutting down flowers and green pieces and stuffing our vases. I looked at the flowers, thinking about how we had just cut off their life source.

Their days were numbered. In a few days they'd dry and wilt, their color would fade. I looked at a golden yellow flower. It was beautiful all on its own but now sitting in the vase next to a green-turning-brown fern, it looked even more beautiful. It looked proud. I realized, too, all these flowers were going to die soon anyway, even if they had stayed in the ground, this late in the year. They needed the sun and the water and the soil. They were reliant on other things to keep them alive, but maybe they were happy to die together.

"Well," Sammy said, looking at me. "I think mine's done."

"Mine too."

We both looked toward the woman and saw that she had fallen asleep. I looked at Sammy wide-eyed. "What do we do?" I whispered.

Sammy shrugged. "I guess we leave?"

"Just leave her?" I asked. I looked back at her. She looked comfortable; I didn't want to wake her. And even though I just met her, it seemed to me that she was someone who wouldn't mind waking up alone.

"Let's leave her a note," Sammy said, gesturing with his chin at the notebook on the table next to her.

I handed him my bouquet and walked over to where she was seated. Carefully, quietly, I picked up the notebook. There was a phone number for someone named Jill, a note that said "pay cable bill October 20" and a rudimentary sketch of a man's face. Her husband, I assumed. I flipped it over to find a blank page. *Thanks for the tour!* I wrote. *You have a beautiful garden.* I held the notebook up so Sammy could see what I wrote, but he shook his head. He couldn't read it from where he stood. I rolled my eyes. Hope to see you around town! I signed my name. I set it back on the table and met Sammy at the gate.

We walked home. Sammy told me about a kid in his class whose parents were emailing him all the time about the kid's grades. I listened to him as he talked, recognizing the care he spoke with about the student. Carrying the flowers in front of me as I walked, I felt like a bride. I thought about the old woman, and how we didn't even get her name. I told Sammy that maybe once the flowers died, we could swing by to drop off her vases.

Joshua Zeitler
EARLY ONSET

Behind the twin wilting lilacs
behind the decaying barn

behind my grandpa's farmhouse
was a cornfield

worked by invisible hired hands.
I remember it as another forbidden

threshold. Once, I crossed it.
I ran deep inside. I lost all sense

of direction, distance, time.
I spun and around me

the past, the future, the possible
paths of escape pinched off

in the middle distance.
I collapsed amid the mudcracks.

The sky gathered
its altostratus underskirts,

kicked up dust dancing
with my prayers.

The wind rattled
as through a rainstick.

An armyworm inched past.
I knew, somehow, about

death, had spent hours lying
on my back in the bathtub,

shivering, pruned, ears submerged
in water we had boiled

in as many mismatched pots and kettles
as could fit on the range, the roar

of my grandmother's confusion
harder and harder to drown.

How did I find my way out
of the cornfield? Truly, I don't know

if I ever dared enter it.

Nathan Lipps
WHEN THEY BOUGHT THE FARM THERE WAS AN ABANDONED APPLE ORCHARD

Removed by now and nearly forgotten
but for this as with this

worn out writing of love
and birds lonely in a greater blue

or heavy on some imaginary branch
especially with this snow beyond

the window and the many friends
quite sad and too far away

my brother in a patient's room
wiping and measuring

while cold insists and he holds
tears and a new heartbreak within

through a twelve hour shift
which is a long time

to not cry wanting to cry
especially in winter

in the North when daylight
blinkers out so quick

Tonight I'll sit in the basement
in front of a cheap tv and try

not to drink too much gin
or think of the long guns

I left back in Michigan
instead slicing a granny smith

and spreading out peanut butter
from the expensive grocery store

that makes people feel good
about being liberal and having money

And I'll think of the farm
my parents bought with money

when my brother and I were quite young
and the haggard orchard

where we pitched misshapen fruit
towards each other and struck them

mid-air with an old baseball bat
the fruit exploding

into a thick haze of good health
what any grocer would gladly sell

and how it could be poetic
but mostly exhausting

the day snowing into night
and the night

Felicia Krol
IN REVERSE

for Tom

I learned today that there is a universe,
parallel to ours, where time moves backward.
Where everything we do is the undoing
of something else. Where Tom's death
was his birth. Where he lay in his bed
at dusk's first light and sucked in a slow,
deep breath. Tomorrow, our friend will find him
with his forehead pressed against the window,
aching for warmer weather.
He'll be working so hard all winter to weaken his knee
in preparation for an injury
that will spur him to skateboard every day.

The day after tomorrow, he'll gather with his family
for Easter. He's thinking of it now,
flipping through photos, smiling at the memories
they've yet to make. He's thankful to be surrounded
by people he loves, and who love him —
he's well aware of his blessings.
He's been like this his entire life, all two days of it.

He will unmake his art and swallow his kindnesses.
He'll pose for pictures that vanish
from the roll, one after another;
he'll steal hugs, back away from parties,
unteach us how to cook and craft, pilfer joy.
In just a few days, he'll rise
from the barn's concrete floor and connect midair
with his board, grinding the flat bar
in reverse. He'll scatter the dirt across the floor
and leave the broom in the corner.
He'll lure shut the heavy wooden door,
draw the key from the lock. Then
he'll stomp the ground clean
on his way to the house, each shoe-shaped hole
swelling with snow, each step

smoothing the crystalline surface
until all that remains is a quiet, unbroken plane,
smooth as window glass,
brilliant in the nearly-setting sun.

34

Lauren Camp
FORCE PROPORTIONAL TO VELOCITY

The sun consoles my neck. We are climbing
toward tree crown. A friend chose this day
because the afternoon's texture is full
of rest. She points to raspberries in a warm mantle
and we pick them, tiny and clung
to prickles. It isn't a feast.
Back when he first moved in,
a nurse taped the medical directives inside
my father's wardrobe: beside shirts,
what should happen to the body
when the Alzheimer's ranged its juice through.
The drupe holds its seed within a fleshy pulp.
It will grow from suckers.
Four years, I knew the future.
And then he was gone.
The sky carries on tireless, another hour.
Tawny woods repeat their sugar.

Gary DeCoker
EVERYTHING IS EVERYTHING

I guided Tilly, our black lab, into the garage for her final trip to the vet, holding up her backside to keep her legs from splaying out. My wife Pam had the hatch of the car open and Tilly crouched down, readying herself for the now impossible jump to her usual place among the blankets and toys. I lifted her into the car as I had been doing for the past few months. She hung limp in my arms as I set her down.

In the parking lot of the vet's office, we opened the hatch. Tilly was leaning far back against the seat, so Pam and I took turns climbing partially into the car to stroke her while we waited for the vet techs to bring the gurney. Tilly's eyes were alert as always, but her body didn't respond. "Tilly's a good girl." "Oh, what a good dog." "We're going to see your friends." Our old phrases sounded a bit frantic, offering comfort to no one.

Two young women pushed a tall metal table on rollers that looked more like an elementary school AV cart than medical equipment. I reached into the car to pull the blanket, and Tilly along with it, to get her where we could reach her. I lifted her back end and somehow the four of us got her on the gurney. As they wheeled her toward the office, Tilly lay calmly, except for a moment when she twisted her neck to look over her shoulder, her left eye rolling back to catch a panicked glimpse of me. I can't delete this image from my memory.

I captured another image that morning with my phone: Tilly lying on her blanket in front of the fireplace during the two hours between our making the appointment and leaving for the vet's office. Her legs stretch out awkwardly from her misshapen hips. She barely moved, even when we petted her.

I look at that photo often. Seeing her in such discomfort reminds me of the weeks preceding her final day when Pam and I struggled to meet her needs—gates on the stairs to keep her from following us, a full-body harness to help her walk outside without falling, blankets on the floor with one of us next to her during the long nights. These thoughts comfort me in knowing that we made the right decision, but her eye, that one glimpse, shatters my certainty.

❋ ❋ ❋ ❋ ❋

Loneliness fills the void of Tilly's absence and I wonder why I feel lonely when Pam sits with me in the same room, eats at the same table, lies in the same bed? Is our nearly 40-year bond not enough to sustain me? Or maybe it's too much, the accumulated conversations that have left nothing unsaid, nothing in need of repeating. Over the last 13 years, Tilly brought new topics. Early on, we negotiated where she would sleep (on the floor in the bedroom), who would walk her (mostly me after Pam tripped on her leash and broke a finger), how strictly to follow her training (in the end Tilly trained us). Routines settled, the conversations turned to the people she met, the squirrels she chased, her single-minded joy in life. And in her last few months, we talked mostly of adjustments as we tried to reclaim that joy by making her comfortable.

Pam and I sit across from each other over morning coffee, Tilly's blanket lying empty, both of us quiet, knowing that any conversation will turn to her and lead us both to tears. The loneliness deepens in Pam's company, and I wonder what it would be like were I living alone.

✽ ✽ ✽ ✽ ✽

Pam called Tilly her "lifetime dog," the one that will live with her forever. "I think I treated her too much like a child," she said, the child we never had. Thirty-some years ago, we exhausted all affordable options in trying to conceive and in the years after found ways to move forward. With or without children, we'd say, we'd be living alone now. Nothing really changed.

But Tilly did change us. We didn't treat her like a child—no pink ribbons or baby talk—but she had needs and we met them. Food, bedding, trips to the vet. Watching Pam provide for Tilly gave me glimpses of her as the mother she never became. Pam says she became too attached, and she's surprised by how attached I must have been. "I've never seen you so emotional. I didn't even think you were that excited about having a dog."

I always thought I would be a good father. My five years as an elementary school teacher and decades teaching college students surely were good preparation. But my confidence seemed unwarranted when up against my actions with Tilly. Sure, I could

be warm and nurturing, but my impatience often dominated. I'd yank
Tilly's leash a bit too hard when she wouldn't follow my verbal cue,
gripe about delayed departures as we prepared things for Tilly, resent
having to clean up a mess when Tilly's stomach emptied on the carpet.

Tilly was a mirror. I treasured what she brought forth in
Pam, but cringed at my reflection when I let life's frustrations impose
themselves. As Tilly got older and less willful, we found our rhythm and
I showed a better side of myself, at least with her. I learned a lot, but her
lessons ended before I had mastered them.

✿ ✿ ✿ ✿ ✿

When our neighbor's dog died and they told us how much they missed
her, I remember Pam saying, "Dogs weave themselves so fully into our
lives." A cliché, I thought at the time, a hollow phrase that people toss
out to ease the awkwardness of grief. But for those first few weeks, we
repeated it almost every day.

Closing the door so she doesn't follow me downstairs, rushing in
from the garage so I meet her on the living room carpet rather than the
slippery hallway floor—I still catch myself altering my behavior only to
confront Tilly's absence, and that instant feels sharp, like a knife poking
the realization deep into me. When it happens, I try to laugh at myself
and recall something pleasant. But those moments pile up, and by day's
end, the grief weighs heavy.

Tilly's life took in a third of our marriage—through retirement,
a move, a vacation condo in Northern Michigan, the births of grand
nieces and nephews, and the death of three of our parents. When my
father died, I told myself his time had come, his life reduced to a few
hundred square feet and a couple dozen medications. Living no longer
offered him anything, I thought, but maybe it was that he no longer
offered anything to me. Tilly spoke to us until the very end.

✿ ✿ ✿ ✿ ✿

It took a few months to get used to having a dog, a third presence
with her own needs and routines. Tilly imposed her schedule and we
adjusted. She thrived on predictability—meals, walks, games, sleep—
and our retired life made it easy for us to follow her lead. Without our
realizing it, she choreographed almost every aspect of our home life,
tweaking the routines as she aged. In recent late evenings, she'd get

38

up from her spot in front of the fireplace and stand staring at Pam, informing her of the day's end.

"You can go to bed," we'd say, and Tilly would head for her blanket in our bedroom. We'd soon follow.

We are still figuring out how to spend Tilly's hours, not sure whether we have too much free time without her or whether we gave up too much time for her. What we do know is without her orchestration, we have no one to guide us as we weave the extra time into an evolving routine.

The larger blocks of time seem easier to fill. In the morning, without her walk and meal, I start writing sooner and stay with it a bit longer. But I miss her visits. She'd nudge my office door open, and I'd get her settled without losing my train of thought. Soon after, I'd stand and we'd go for a walk, my stiff back grateful for the stretch.

But it is in the day's transitions where I most feel her loss. From the office to the kitchen to the bathroom, back to the office, onward through the day from one thing to the next, it was in these gaps between activities that I would look for Tilly. I was checking on her, I told myself, but really I was after the wag of her tail, the glint in her eye, the comfort of her presence.

❋ ❋ ❋ ❋ ❋

I walked Tilly five or six times a day, more than she needed, but it fulfilled both of us. Out the front door, we'd turn left toward the pond, along the path, and back onto the street. There weren't many options: the neighborhood walkers moved either clockwise or counterclockwise. When Tilly got to the pond, she'd sometimes raise her nose, sniff the air, and then abruptly turn around. A few minutes later her favorite dog-loving couple would appear around the corner. Or if I saw them first, I'd say, "Let's say hi," and Tilly would jump to attention like a bird dog.

If a stranger appeared, her pace was slower, but her enthusiasm was the same. Her eyes would light up and tail wag as she searched for a dog-friendly sign. She was a master manipulator, a salesperson whose only item was herself and whose only currency was attention. I stood by, answering questions. "Ten years old but thinks she's a puppy." "A labradoodle that got shorted on the doodle." "She spent six weeks at a woman's penitentiary being trained to be a service dog, but she flunked out. Too social."

I enjoyed the comfortable repetition of those conversations, and they often led to sharing something more about families, friends, and foibles. On our trips to Michigan, Pam and I took turns walking Tilly while the other went into a store or a bathroom or a gas station. Tilly would keep an eye on the entrance while at the same time greeting passersby. On our first trip without Tilly, I tired of the grocery store, so I walked around the parking lot, occasionally peering into the store looking for Pam. People snuck glances at me as they maneuvered to put distance between us. "Let's say hi," I wanted to shout. "I'm the one who used to walk Tilly."

❊ ❊ ❊ ❊ ❊

For the first few weeks, Pam insisted on leaving Tilly's things in place — jars of treats on the counter, her bedding here and there, blankets in the back of the car. Gradually, she started putting things away, but she kept Tilly's favorite blanket next to our bed and even took it on an overnight trip. It smells like Tilly, she said.

After a month or so, we went around the house gathering up Tilly's belongings. Some things went into boxes in the garage; most went to the Humane Society. Each item contained a memory. The cloth crate we tried to use in a hotel brought the image of Tilly's head poking out of the top of the crate through an opening she had found in the zipper. The ball we threw over and over when she was young reminded us of her love of running. And these memories connected to events. We were at that hotel on a trip to Grand Rapids for one of Pam's exhibitions. And we remembered throwing the ball while waiting for family and friends at my parents' house in their small Lake Huron town as we gathered in celebration of my father's life of eighty-nine years.

So much took place during our time with Tilly, and through it all, Pam and I became a stronger couple with more feeble bodies, ready to assume the role of the oldest members of our extended families. In "dog years" Tilly lived past ninety, but for us it was thirteen, a significant duration no matter how you calculate. Maybe what I'm mourning isn't Tilly at all, but the passing of time. In thirteen years, I'll be only a few years from ninety.

❊ ❊ ❊ ❊ ❊

My friends in college had a phrase that we jokingly used when life overwhelmed us. "Everything is everything," we'd say, not knowing what we meant, other than acknowledging that under our adolescent confidence, we didn't have a clue. Tilly's life clearly marked the last thirteen years and, as I try to make sense of it, all I can come up with is that she was right there with us, her presence now as vivid a part of our memories as the people, the places, the emotions.

This spring we took Tilly's ashes with us to our summer condo in Leelanau County. We planned to spread them near her favorite Lake Michigan beach. As we unpacked the car upon arrival, our neighbor came up the hill, her dog barking as it pulled ahead on a long leash. We greeted neighbor and dog, then went inside. "Funny," Pam said, "I was carrying the bag with Tilly's ashes up the stairs instead of her running up ahead of me." I took a deep breath. "Everything is everything."

Casey Jo Graham Welmers
ALL MY LITTLE PURGATORIES

I.
At age five and under cover of night, I fold myself into a crisscross shape as my nose bleeds crimson, transforming my nightgown into a bright cotton poinsettia. I'm slouched outside the bathroom, the door wide open, light fixture beaming into my half-moon eyelids. I sense the universe tilting in a dangerous sort of way, so despite my full bladder and bloody nose I remain stock-still, my breath held. The universe is always tilting, but most of the time you don't see it and most of the time it doesn't matter. Now the universe is sideways and upside down. The buzzing light fixture crashes from the ceiling, ignites the linoleum in a whoosh of green and orange flames. I bleed, the floor burns, and the universe twists into my mouth and peels a scream from my stained lips. Two parent apparitions appear into the fire and blood, staunching both. The fire singes a kidney bean-shaped hole into the plastic floor and also into my hippocampus. For the next 40 years I will pick at these shapes, the first with my toe, the second with my memory. My mom pinches my nose with a cloud of Kleenex and asks how I knew not to go into the bathroom. I don't know how to tell her about the universe being so tipsy that night.

II.
Creation, upon sensing my mom's desire to keep me tucked away in perpetuity, shakes me from the vault of her belly a month ahead of schedule by placing her in a minor car accident. The bumper of her red Gremlin crumples, her water breaking across the vinyl interior. My father's knees buckle, and he weaves into a world of scintillating light when tasked with cutting my umbilical cord. So physically sensitive to the ambulations of the universe is he, no doubt detecting the scales of his own life recalibrating violently with the responsibility of parenthood. Clearly, I'm not the only member of my family prone to this shake, rattle, and roll. Does the shifting of the cosmos sometimes make us so wobbly that we stop to brace ourselves? Or do we pause because our animal senses alert us when shifting is imminent? Perhaps a mix of both. Others might find these pauses to be small purgatories: boring liminal spaces interrupting the action sequences of their lives. I generally prefer to linger in them while the universe performs osteomancy on my still flesh-covered bones, skittering them across unseen dimensions, divining the future in my

scattered limbs. Seated in lotus position while my nose bleeds is not the only time I've had premonitions of things yet-to-pass. I find myself hesitant to step into the next minutes and weeks and years of my life, afraid I'll have missed something written on the floors or the walls of my arrested spaces. I fear the universe will tilt too far or too fast, that my bones will be tossed so hard they'll shatter and turn to dust before I can make sense of any of it.

III.
Where I pause my sister accelerates, rocketing through her life clear to the other side of the universe, somewhere beyond any tilting and shifting. At 16 she leaves home, at 21 she marries, at 22 she divorces. At 40 years old she dies of a highly aggressive colon cancer. After her diagnosis I sink into my leaf-littered lawn, legs crossed, fingers splayed. I watch her turn her face to the sun and laugh and want to stay paused right here forever, because I know what is coming and because all of creation is now tipping so fiercely that I'm violently ill. All of my little purgatories are now tiny heavens and tiny hells. In these pauses I relish her existence with a heat that borders on burning while anticipatory grief gnaws out jagged segments of my core. We exhaust western medicine, wildly potent THC suppositories, a drug meant to kill parasites, acupuncture, a Peruvian shaman. I'm down on my knees and it's just like a prayer but it's so not Madonna; it's me with my eyes closed tight, begging the universe for stillness, or at bare minimum, a certain kind of grace. Two weeks before she dies, my sister tells me that in her last session with the shaman she felt an intense shifting, *the universe, perhaps?* I am a seismograph registering an earthquake, something I imagine a 90s actor from a B movie referring to as the 'Big One.' This kind of shifting I understand. Her death breaks my purgatory languishing. I'm left with a fervent drive to rip through time and space, daring the universe to throttle me. Although I flail forward, I remain suspended in time to the hour and minute she left. My ghost feet are mired to the muted blue place where her hands and eyes flutter toward the stars; her mouth becomes a cipher, and I hold my breath.

Carolyn Fay
MOM LUNCH

"That's your lunch?"

Bea was crumbling a burnt piece of bacon over cornbread spread with olive hummus. Hubby and the kids had leftover spaghetti and meatballs. One meatball each for the kids. Hubby got three. There wasn't enough for Bea to have a portion. She shrugged. "It's part of the job."

"Mommy's lunch is weird!" Kid #1's mouth was a cave of mashed meatball. A meatball Bea had carefully formed the night before.

"Weeird," echoed Kid #2. Spaghetti sauce freckled her cheeks.

When Bea was their age, her mother ate weird lunches. Ricotta cheese and jelly on a waffle. Bologna wrapped around chicken salad. Bea at nine, ten, eleven would dip her spoon in her tomato soup and vow softly to the ghost of the grilled cheese that she would never eat like that when she was a mother. She would eat proper lunches. Tomato soup and grilled cheese. Baked beans and hot dogs. Spaghetti and meatballs.

Now here she was, biting into a hummus-slathered, bacon-dotted cornbread monstrosity. She recognized that the flavors and textures clashed. That she could and perhaps should spit it out. Let the kids see what *that* looked like.

Except Bea got a strange kick out of finishing stuff nobody else wanted.

Ravioli and half a hot dog. Goulash over grits. A dollop of tuna fish salad with fried rice. The heel of a meatloaf on an everything bagel.

Hubby said, "You're a leftover artiste."

The specific combinations didn't matter to Bea. She remembered how her father would mix his food together on his plate until it resembled a masticated mash of gray gruel. "Who cares?" he'd say. "It's all going to the same place."

Bea shivered when she found a single dill-pickle chip left in the jar. She set it on top of an almond butter Swiss cheese sandwich. Delicious.

Why had no one ever told her about this? She figured women kept it secret. If men knew, they'd try to co-opt or control it. *The sisterhood of Mom Lunch.* She liked the idea.

Grandma came to visit. This was Bea's mother. Bea made a proper lunch for the kids and Grandma. Her own lunch was leftover sauteed zucchini and half a tin of sardines.

"Mom Lunch," she said to Grandma. A beatific smile blossomed on Bea's face, what she hoped would function as a wink to her mother, who would understand and nod appreciatively, acknowledging the sisterhood, like when 12-year-old Bea brought her a pair of crimson-stained panties.

Grandma glanced at the limp, overheated zucchini draped over the sardines and wrinkled her nose, as though adult Bea had just thrust a blood-soaked maxi pad in her face.

"I always hated eating leftovers," she said. "There's no point in bothering. Just throw them out, Bea. Throw them out."

❅ ❅ ❅ ❅ ❅

Bea was sewing a button onto Kid #2's jacket. It was a red plastic button with four little holes in the center. Instead of poking the needle through one of the holes, she popped the button into her mouth and gulped it down whole.

That night, after flossing her teeth, she swallowed the long minty strand of floss.

Now she was smearing butter on a torn playing card. The queen of hearts. The butter was soft. The playing card was stiff. It resisted Bea's teeth but the butter made it soggy enough to crumple and fold into her mouth.

"Bea, this has to stop," Hubby said.

She learned to sneak stray things into her mouth. The junk drawer in the kitchen opened into an all-she-can-eat buffet. She found a plastic rosary she had as a child. Pink. Nestled inside a small plastic egg. She remembered her grandmother on her deathbed cramming her own rosary into her mouth, choking on the crucifix.

"She had dementia," Bea's mother had said. "She didn't know what she was doing."

Didn't she? Bea knew her plastic rosary would taste like sugar and incense. She kept the rosary in her pocket.

Bea's mother invited her out to lunch. A fancy lunch at a new restaurant. Bea wondered if this was her mother's way of coming round, of acknowledging the ancient sisterhood. They would share an appetizer right down to the garnish. They would carve off shavings of the candle and slip them under their tongues as though they were mints.

If not, Bee had the rosary egg. It lay against her thigh in her pants pocket.

But when Bea entered the restaurant, the host led her to a large circular table. Her mother was there, along with Hubby and the kids, plus her brother and her sister-in-law.

"What is this, a surprise party?"

Hubby pulled a chair out for her, all courtesy with his shirt tucked in. "Yeah, Bea, something like that."

There were water glasses in front of everyone but no menus. The kids weren't even squirming. Then she realized they were playing games on Hubby's phone.

"Okay, so, what are we here for?"

"A family luncheon," Grandma said. "We're here to eat. It's all on me." She waved a heavily ringed, wrinkly hand and two waiters appeared with dishes of food.

So much food. A gorgeous plate of salmon sat in front of Bea, with crisp potatoes, and a handful of green beans dotted with tiny diced red peppers.

"Sofrito sauce," said one of the waiters. The other waiter brought her an iced tea. There were hot rolls. Butter sculpted into the shape of tiny chickens.

"Eat up," Grandma said. Kid #1 and #2 dug into big bowls of spaghetti, sauce already dripping down their faces. No one else was eating. The adults watched Bea.

She recognized the beauty of the food and its enticing aroma, but it seemed to her like a simulacra of food on her plate. Not something she could actually eat.

It's not what she wanted.

"Go on, honey," Hubby whispered. "Try it."

Bea fidgeted with her napkin. She eyed the salt shaker and the crumbs on the table cloth where Kid #2 had ripped into her roll. The crumbs looked good. The crumbs she could eat. Or the strands of spaghetti Kid #1 didn't finish. He never cleaned his plate. He was incapable of it.

"Just one bite," Hubby said. "It's delicious."

The other adults made murmurous noises of assent as they dipped their forks into their meals, testing the water, and when the water turned out to be fine, they chowed down. Bea's stomach rumbled. She was hungry, but not for salmon in sofrito sauce. She reached for the rosary egg in her pocket, felt the smooth contours of it.

"Oh for God's sake, Bea, eat! It's a proper meal. You can eat a proper meal." Grandma slammed her knife and fork down on the table. Spit and sauce gathered in the corners of her mouth. "You are not a garbage pail."

Everyone looked up at that—Hubby, both kids, brother, and sister-in-law. Hubby fit the fork and knife into her hands, as though maybe she had forgotten how to use utensils.

She had not forgotten. Bea watched the sauce dry on her mother's cheek. She clocked the tremor in her mother's hand. All this time, her mother had misunderstood. It's not that she kept Bea out of the sisterhood. She just didn't understand. She didn't understand anything.   Garbage pail? Is that what she thought?

Bea looked around the table. None of them saw her for what she was.

"I'm not a garbage pail," she said. She felt Hubby beside her relax, like a lawn ornament deflating.

"Thank you for lunch." She cut a hefty chunk of salmon and speared it, along with a potato, and a green bean on her fork.

Everyone, even the kids, held their breaths until she put the food in her mouth, chewed, and swallowed.

Now everyone was deflated lawn ornaments. There was clinking and laughing and the waiters refilled the glasses.

Bea took a second bite. And a third.

"Oh thank goodness, honey," Hubby said.

"It's good, isn't it?" said her sister-in-law.

Bea nodded, though she barely registered the taste of the food. The plastic pink rosary lay warm in her pocket, like a lit cigarette.

Grandma had her eye on Bea. Bea swallowed the last bite of salmon.

She was no garbage pail. She took a swig of iced tea.

She was a comet, gathering ice and debris, swirling and growing larger.

Her family didn't see that she could take it all in. The leftovers, the broken bits and bobs, the torn playing cards, the holey socks, Hubby's admonitions, the kids' whining, her mother's judgmental glances—all the detritus that collected around her. She could eat it all. Of course she could eat their salmon and sofrito sauce with the crisp potatoes and the green beans. *What else you got?*

"You did great, honey," Hubby was saying. "I knew you could do it. I knew you were okay, deep down."

Deep down she was a solid core of ice. Now they were serving hot fudge sundaes. The kids squealed with delight. Bea was glad they were getti what they wanted. The kids, Hubby, her mother, the family—they were all getting what they wanted. Thanks to her. For them, Bea would plunge her spoon into the congealed fudge and pull it out all dripping and gooey with ic cream and chocolate and wrap her tongue around it. It's not what she wante to eat. But since when did moms get to eat exactly what they wanted? If Bea were still feeling romantic about it, she might think that was the whole point of this intervention-lunch—her mother's way of reminding her that she didn have a choice. Wouldn't that be amazing if that was her mother's idea all alo

Bea laughed out loud at the thought.

"Something funny?" Hubby asked.

"Mommy wants another dessert!" the kids screamed, chocolate sauc and milky ice cream spraying from their lips.

"Do you?" Grandma gave Bea the once-over, the way she used to wh Bea was a teenager getting dressed to go out.

Bea's hunger gnawed her insides.

"I couldn't possibly eat another bite." She fingered the rosary in her pocket. "I can't remember the last time I felt so full."

She was big enough for the lie. She was blazing through the sky.

Grandma sat back in her chair as though she herself were finally full the expression on her face a collage of deeply smug and deeply relieved.

They left the restaurant together, the whole family, arm in arm—the kids, sugar-stuffed and wild, and Hubby with the heavy-lidded look that me he was already thinking about something else. Later, Bea would eat a cigare stub she picked up in the parking lot. And some loose change. The rosary, sh save for a special occasion.

"Bea," Grandma said, "From now on, eat real food. No more garbag You're worth more than that."

Bea swallowed the back-handed compliment. The kids tugged her d the sidewalk. They were oblivious, obnoxious, and happy. Their laughter tas like sticky lemonade on the sole of a rubber flip-flop.

Felicia Krol
MINUTES

for Shea

I'd take them all if they'd come to me,
gather them in unmanageable amounts, scooping whole-armed
from the tile or pavement or wherever, chest-to-floor and unshaken
by my own greed. Fill every space with them—the boxes and boxes
we still haven't unpacked, the cupboards that don't quite latch.
Pile them onto the couch to fold later with the towels. After dark,
we'd brush them into each other's hair; stir them into soup.
Lie awake in bed and hold them wide open, flipping their seconds like pages
marked with every possible doing. Can you imagine?
Stretching them slow to their fibers; draping from the ceiling; wrapped
around the banister. Spilling over, drawers bursting—we'd scatter them
into steaming new bathwater with lavender and honey, climb in laughing.
We'd light every candle and kiss our mouths numb.

Stefanie Lee
HANDLE WITH CARE

Do not seize the day. It does not like to be seized. It is not a bouquet or a naughty child. It is a damp-mouthed thing, pacing behind the chicken wire of your intentions. The day startles easily. A loud hope will make it flatten its ears, bristle its clocks, bark back the sun from your windowsill. You must not reach for it too abruptly. Let the day come to you like a feral thing—rain-boned, mistrusting, covered in dewy light. Keep your movements vague. Speak in lowercase. Some mornings, the day sniffs your hand. You call this progress. It may allow a slow brushing of your knuckles against its flank. The fur is soft here. You remember your mother's kitchen towel—damp with lemon, too kind for the mess it endured. But if the day stiffens, if it bares its heat or lurches sideways with that sudden flame of unfinished grieving— you must not chase it. You are not owed its softness. Let it slink back into the treeline of chipped plates, half-written emails. Trust softness to find you like relics find ruin: late, deliberate, on the cliffside of collapse. There is no shame in retreat. The bedspread is still warm. You may return to it like a widow to the sea. Some days are not meant to be touched. They bruise easily. They bloom best along the periphery—watch them shimmer at the edge of your stillness, a kind of grace that arrives only when you stop demanding it.

Sheila Black
AUGUST

My heart feels so still. Only the grackles
and finches outside on the deck,
Morning's bleach and to watch it
arrive a little later each day. Inside
for months, we view the world
through a scrim: bluish dragonfly,
carmine bougainvillea which sprouts
as if trying to devour the fence.
I can see stars even as the sky lightens,
their peculiar fixity—a burning
that never stops or at least not in any
time I can follow. You've stocked
the house again—the gluten-free bread,
the big jars of peanut butter and honey,
a bag of slightly wizened apples.
I should notice more the care you
take—middle-of-the-night trips
to the drug store to get me cough syrup
or Tampax. A constancy of stars.
The wind shifts, the leaves lift, rustle.
Who will remember our traceless
civilization—rituals of walking the dog,
wasting Sundays with television?
Deeper things only you and I saw:
green herons colonizing the cedar,
hunting the neighbor's kittens,
our child dying at birth, then jolted
back to life, infused with blood from a chilled
storeroom. I want to believe in a God
that is simply the record of all things,
as a leaf is veined or a stone pocked
with the record of each ice age, each
summer-of-all-the-forests-burning.

Kat Moore
SISTERS AT NIGHT

After the painting Moonstricken Girls, by Carroll Cloar

Purple blooms everywhere. Wildflowers, viola, echinacea, creep across
the field and twine up trees, purpling the leaves. The moon glows
orange tonight. Sara darts through the field singing a song she made
up. Louise is behind her, skipping along to Sara's tune. Sisters. Ages 9
and 13. The only ones who know that each night their dad leans a little
too much, smells like antiseptic used to treat one of their cuts when
they go too fast and skid their bikes on the pavement. Or that their
mother washes the dishes by hand to give her something to do other
than tend to her daughters or husband, and that often, a plate slips,
shatters, and the mother groans a little too long, her face turned toward
the water trickling out the spout, until she smiles toward the girls, and
laughs, "Oh, my slippery fingers." Louise always sweeps up the pieces.

Louise and Sara love this bruise of night, this track of grass
behind their house, and they hurry to the trees to lounge and dance,
and let nature take them away for a little while. Sara likes to listen to
Louise talk of middle school, boys, and of this one girl with magenta
hair. When Louise says her name, her cheeks flush. But tonight, in the
middle of the field, Louise in her lavender sweater, Sara a step ahead,
the purple is too much, clashes with the orange from the moon, these
colors of fire and wound. Louise's legs tremor and hips swing, her head
spins, and she clasps her hands to her hair. She can hear the crickets
chirping, and can feel the pull of pomegranate from the land. And
Sara, the youngest, always wanting to be like her big sister, mimics
Louise, hoping the magic of thirteen will dust her skin tonight, dip her
in violet, and that the moon will come down from its perch, and tell her
the secrets of girls, about the desire Louise already feels budding inside
her shimmering limbs.

Ian Day
PAST WHEN I'M DEAD

When we went to Húsafell Hot Springs
and our guide looked like a young Sue Perkins
and we got on a white bus with nine women
from Iceland—it was their birthday—all of them
were childhood friends from a long time ago
and they all looked like a perfect grandmother
and we took off our clothes and got in the water
it was warm but not hot and we stepped in
the river and it was ice cold glacier water,
Sue Perkins told us we were real Vikings.
I liked that.

We drove off-road in a Toyota Aygo despite what
I promised to the car rental company.
In the middle of a rocky field, an Irishman took
us down a frozen cave made from ancient lava
and he pointed to a ledge we couldn't see:
there's a real Viking down here dead with glass
beads and a sword and the remnants of a fire.
We never found his bones but we know he's here:
an outcast who probably drove off-road.
We go as deep as we go and the Irishman says
here's the end of the road turn off all the lights
now and be very quiet and one at a time
make a sound whatever sound you want so
of course there's a scream but I cup my hands
together to make a birdsong and I'm so excited
I make a farting sound instead.

I want to find the words that don't exist: the ones
that say I want to be buried here with our
scattered Viking bones mixed up all together
and our glass beads so everyone knows
we never left but were never found like a
birdsong underground.

Morgan Rose-Marie
WE SPREAD

I cannot say I'm surprised that I learn the news of my mother's impending heart surgery from my sister. I also learned about my mother's disappointment with my wedding and about her first trip overseas from my sister, Stephanie. But this is not something we like to talk about.

***** *

Two days after my mother's surgery, I meet Pando. He is an aspen tree whose acquaintance I've wanted to make for more than a decade — perhaps longer. Before, I just didn't know he existed. Before, I just wished something like Pando was possible.

My mother-in-law is visiting my wife and me in Utah, and for this, we've elected to drive two and a half hours south to see the aspen tree of all aspen trees. It is October, and the colors are changing even here in the mountains. Pando is a midday sun when I see him. Every leaf is gold. He's breathtaking if you know what you're looking at and, I think, even if you don't. My mouth is a perfect "o" as I take in this God on earth.

But my mother-in-law confesses her disappointment as we return home: "I thought it'd be...*more?*"

***** *

Steph discovered our mother's trip abroad accidentally. A shared Amazon Prime account. An outlet adapter ordered on it. She sent a text with a screenshot: *why'd u buy this?*

The explosion that followed between them was more powerful than any that might have come from a phone-frying spark or consequential power outage.

Steph realized our mother had meant this to be a secret. A secret international vacation on which my mother was taking our two other sisters. She wasn't going to tell us until after they returned. Or, more likely, until pictures of them were inevitably discovered.

***** *

When imagining the largest tree, I picture something like the General Sherman Tree, a sky-high sequoia with impressive girth. Pando isn't that. No single trunk, or *stem*, in the colony is particularly tall or wide. But Pando comprises about 47,000 stems covering more than 100 acres. These stems may look like individual trees, but they are connected by a massive root system. Single stems may—and do—die, and genetically identical ones replace them.

As we walk through Pando, I keep reminding myself that each stem is not a tree in the way I am apt to think of a tree. Each trunk may be more akin to an arm.

I put my hand on one. I wonder if the pressure, the heat of my palm travels through the roots to the rest of the clones, the other limbs. In touching this trunk, am I touching them all? It feels like I am. I shiver and become a trembling aspen myself for just a moment before I hurry to catch up with my wife and her mother on the trail ahead.

They have a relationship I doubt I'll fully understand, but I continue to observe with interest. They speak on the phone every day. Sometimes when my wife is bored, she'll call a second or third time. This has been their pattern forever, it seems.

When I started college, I spoke so infrequently to my mother the first semester that she finally sent an email asking, "Are you alive???"

This has been our pattern.

❈ ❈ ❈ ❈ ❈

In my late twenties in graduate school, I traveled to Ireland and visited the house in Dublin where my great-grandfather grew up. It had become a small bed and breakfast and felt like home. After that, Steph suggested we take a family trip to Ireland in lieu of our usual Christmas. She suggested this every year until now.

Mom finally took her suggestion, just not her. Or me. Though I haven't seen any pictures, I have seen one short video—a clip secretly captured—of our younger sister Sydney berating my mother on a verdant hill in the Irish countryside. Beside them, a crumbling castle.

❈ ❈ ❈ ❈ ❈

Brian Doyle wrote about hearts best:

*No living being is without interior liquid motion. We all churn inside…
When young we think there will come one person who will answer and sustain
us always; when we are older we know this is the dream of a child, that all
hearts finally are bruised and scarred, scored and torn, repaired by time and
will, patched by force of character, yet fragile and rickety forevermore…*

The news that my mother will have surgery on her heart stops
my own. And then, before it can return to normal, there is a second skip
brought on by the question of whether she will share this news with me
herself—I have doubt, just for a second, but it is there.

❀ ❀ ❀ ❀ ❀

When Steph called my mother, aghast that this international trip was
planned without including her, let alone informing her, the conversation
clotted.

Several of my mother's coworkers had been diagnosed with cancer
in the last couple years. If my mother wasn't next, she was, at least, made
suddenly and very painfully aware of mortality.

My sister has traveled quite a bit: Iceland, Hawaii…Couldn't my
mother take a trip for herself? She'd dedicated her entire existence to her
kids. Couldn't she do anything for herself for once? She didn't have much
time left.

How much time did she have left?

"She basically told me she regrets being our mother," Steph
whisper-cried on the phone later that night.

That cannot be, I thought. All my mother's ever wanted, the only
thing she's ever wanted was to be a mom. Now that her nest is empty,
when she's not working, she just fills the time, she says. This saddens
Steph and me. Find something you love. Do something for you, we've both
urged. And then she did.

Maybe she does regret motherhood, I thought again. Because, I
worried, can you love what destroys you?

Her devotion to her daughters contributed to her divorce. My
father's parting letter: "Everything is one big sacrifice for the kids. If you
could sacrifice some of your time with them…"

Her sole identity as mother has contributed to her current
depression: if she isn't a perfect mother, then who is she?

I fear her commitment to one volatile daughter, Sydney, may be
killing her.

56

When I first recognized this, I started to doubt I'd want to
be a mother myself. My friend Megan would have been a wonderful
mother, if she'd lived long enough to become one. She gave more to
our shared students than I ever could, than I ever wanted to.

❊ ❊ ❊ ❊ ❊

It was Megan who taught me about aspen trees, informed me of
Pando when I was just out of college and we were both working as
high school teachers, our first real jobs. Over Christmas that year, she
learned she had cancer. She went into remission several months later
but did not return to school; eventually, I left too.

During those years, I practiced mixed martial arts. Five days a
week, sometimes six, and sometimes twice a day if the dojo's schedule
allowed. Then I went to the gym to work out.

One morning working my biceps at the gym, in the short space
between one song and another, I heard the two women at the machine
behind me: I wouldn't want my arms to look like *that.*

Blood flushed my cheeks, but I didn't stop the exercise. In
high school and college, I'd cared so much about how people saw me
that, like many adolescent girls, I struggled with disordered eating.
After almost a decade of recovery, I wasn't thinking about how my
body looked but rather what it could do.

I had finally made my body mine.

As a child, I'd pretended to be any and every animal I had a
costume nose for and even those I didn't. I ran around on all fours
until a ganglion cyst swelled on the back of my hand. Now, I was on
my hands and knees on the floor again. I rolled on the mats, wrapping
my arms around necks and capturing limbs to lock their joints and
force surrender. In jiu-jitsu, this is called submission.

The heart is a muscle. Just like the others I'd torn in order to
build. It stands to reason that a hurt heart becomes stronger after it
heals. It does have to heal first, though.

❊ ❊ ❊ ❊ ❊

Pando doesn't have a heart. But trees do have a pulse, because, yes,
we all churn inside. Pando's bark contracts and expands, a life-giving
muscle, pumping water up and out to the golden leaves. And the

leaves in turn are ready to shiver a song and energy down down down to its shared roots.

If the bark of one stem pumps nutrients to the roots that the entire colony shares, I wonder what the individual stem risks to sustain the whole.

❈ ❈ ❈ ❈ ❈

I always enjoyed when my mother read *The Giving Tree* to us as kids. It was only as an adult that I learned how much she hated that book.

I, too, resist the story: a tree who sacrifices so much of itself that, in the end, it is left a stump, and, even then, it is used without reciprocation by the boy who has taken everything else.

It's so easy to see the tree as woman, as mother, and this only disturbs me more.

I do not want my life to require the sacrifice of another. I do not want my mother to give so much of herself to anyone—myself included—that she has nothing left for herself.

While I doubt my mother-in-law feels this way, I see her openly wish she could have given my wife more in childhood, even do more for her now. I fear that to be a mother is to become the stump or, at least, to wish to become the stump.

If I become a mother, I will not become a stump, even for my own children.

It seems my mother may feel like she has.

❈ ❈ ❈ ❈ ❈

For a long time, we believed trees competed with each other for resources. We were wrong. Neither of these facts surprises me though.

The American cowboys *broke* horses—running them into the ground, into submission. Today, many of these original methods are considered abuse. Today, we seek to teach horses through their own language.

I've learned the language of horses, and I would like to better understand the language of trees. Both are a kind of body talk.

Trees speak through the underground "wood-wide web," a symbiotic relationship between their roots and fungi called the mycorrhizal network. Their most frequent message is one of cooperation. They share nutrients and resources. They warn each other of drought and disease. They may even recognize kinship.

❄❄❄❄❄

That short video from Ireland isn't the only one of its kind.

I do not get along with my sister Sydney—she was invited to Ireland, so I was not. I could tell you about how she calls me "bitch" without provocation or how she has at least once put hands on our mother when things didn't go her way, or how she got so drunk at my wedding that I asked my mother to remove her and my mother drove her away from the reception—missing part of it herself. I'd learn weeks later that this ruined my wedding for my mother because we couldn't all be happy together. Because I'd asked for my sister to be taken away, the fault was mine.

Perhaps the fault lies not in our stars nor in ourselves but in something even closer to the ground, deeper in the earth.

And what if fault is not the only thing buried there in those roots?

❄❄❄❄❄

Pando is Latin for *I spread*. And Pando does indeed. He spreads across his hundred acres. His roots spread resources across thousands of stems. He spreads across time.

Pando is between 9,000 and 14,000 years old, or so the estimates have it. He has not been around forever. Will he be around forevermore?

He could be, but it's unlikely. Not the way the planet is going. Not thanks to us.

This iteration of immortality isn't true immortality. Pando can die, as all living things can and do. But he won't die the way we do. If a disease takes one stem, he'll produce another. Any tumors he develops cannot metastasize. His heart will never stop.

❄❄❄❄❄

If you close your eyes while the wind blows, the forest becomes a river. It's why we call Pando a *quaking* aspen. The wind makes his branches shiver, a woodwind instrument quivering a symphony.

59

Megan taught me this about aspen trees when I visited her at home in Alaska where the species is abundant. *Immortal,* she smiled as she described the clonal colony.

In a few years, her remission ended. For me, she became the aspen. When I hear one quaking, I hear her voice whispering *immortal* among the leaves. When I close my eyes in the windy river Pando plays, I see her face in his chalky bark, young and somehow wiser still.

✿ ✿ ✿ ✿ ✿

My mother's heart surgery is successful. This news comes from her. Over the course of a few hours, a surgeon implants a single stint to alleviate three blockages. She doesn't even have to stay overnight. Her right arm, where they entered, is sore for a couple days, but for the first time in months, she feels normal.

"When you go for your physical, get your cholesterol checked," she instructs. Even now her focus is on her daughters.

I already know my numbers are high, but I don't share this. I will soon start medication. Just like the hypothyroidism I have inherited from her, this condition is genetic. It is something my mother and her mother and father and their mothers and fathers have passed down to me through my family's roots.

We have bad hearts.

✿ ✿ ✿ ✿ ✿

I want children. I didn't always know this, but I know it now. I am, of course, still terrified of what this will take of me. Of what I will give.

I'm sure many mothers worry they will not give enough. I worry, though, that I will not want to give enough, and that what I will give will be my doom.

And still, I want this. To be a mother. To spread, knowing that I will lose parts of myself along the way that I will not recover. Perhaps motherhood is its own kind of immortality, the closest we can come to being eternal.

Jim Daniels

SQUINTING

We take a short walk, my father and I,
following his usual path through the park.
Two men my age sit on a bench day-drinking
with a woman leaning on a stroller
that contains a large colorful parrot.
They greet my father by name.
He introduces me, the visiting son.
They admire his fitness at 95. How old
are you, around 70? one asks me.
68, I say. All my father's old friends
have died. Every day's a class reunion
for him, the woman laughs. We all do.
Is she flirting? He's switched to suspenders.
He stretches their elastic. Sunny spring day,
they're all so happy it almost breaks
my heart or makes me want to puke.
That's some parrot, I say. A hawk drifts
on the wind above us. We all squint up at it.
Even the bird in its cage.

Christine Rhein
AT EIGHTY-FIVE, MY FATHER PHONES
TO TELL ABOUT HIS DAY

"So nice and warm. I drove to the park,
    sat on a bench. Another old guy

was sitting one bench over. I watched
    the birds hunt for crumbs,

the people walking by me. It happened
    so fast—one minute, sparrows

at my feet—the next, a young woman—
    standing there, looking pretty,

and handing me a rose. A white rose.
    Before I could say thank you—

she was gone. I asked the other guy
    if he got a flower too. He said no—

it was only me. She picked me. I mean
    I couldn't stop smiling.

It didn't matter—my hand tremor.
    I didn't care if the petals shook.

When I got home, I dug in the cupboards,
    found an old vase. It's chipped—

nothing fancy anymore. But the rose—
    not a single thorn—looks good."

Camille Newsom
HUMAN SONG

We'd like to roughhouse
handsomely, like the birds.
Even the left-behinds jazz-call
while the sparkplugs of the world
scrap melody onto time, singing
the thoughts of wind. Before this,
before appointments with casseroles
and noise, was pleasure stale?
Or were the aches of fatherhood
and salvaging barns cool-packed
with sequins twisting us, cooing?
What made the silence disappear first?
When will it be time to ratchet
the wrench, to imagine mother
as compost, to leave this world,
only to stir as heart music,
giving, and only giving?

*Note: All words from this poem are borrowed from Phillip Stirling's poem titled
"One Speaks of Loss"*

Kathleen McGookey
ALL DAY, THE HOUSE WREN CALLS

the same loud chattering trill, over and over, because it's trying to nest and attract a mate, but each evening, my husband removes and scatters the tightly packed twigs wrapped with cobwebs and dandelion fluff, my husband who believes the wooden house nailed under the eave of the barn isn't meant for wrens. Crisp and precise, the wren scribbles its notes over my days, as I cook eggs and fold clothes, as I read and nap. It's a battle on a very small scale: in two minutes my husband undoes a day's work. Does the wren pause each morning, puzzled or annoyed, to find its nest gone, once again? Or does it blink, cock its head, and listen to instinct, which says simply, *begin*.

Fleda Brown
MY WORLD

A woman in old fashioned swim cap, knees bent,
arms behind her, is holding a disk
that holds a round candle. She could dive off
my six-tier bookcase, but she doesn't. The candle
doesn't roll off. Some days she wants to dive so bad,
the world reels. Other days she holds her position
with grace, her thighs strong as steel, steadied
on her wooden base, blue as water. I can't stand
her doing nothing when things are so dire out here.
Maybe there's more than what appears.
There's a threat these days, even if you don't move
a muscle. You can't disappear, and you can't
get rid of the unlit candle that weighs like a bomb
at your back. You may be waiting for things to change,
you may be calculating the distance you could
throw the candle. You know how far down it is.
You don't want to splinter your delicate
arrangement. This is the poem I have for today,
holding safely to the left margin.

Eric Weil
SHUSH

I wander neighborhood cul-de-sacs at dawn,
obeying an impulse to rise and move. Maybe
a fog will lighten soon, like lifting
a mask. From the easement between streets,
a barred owl calls. Maybe the sun stirs

the trees. Garage doors open, cars cough
like patients in waiting rooms, drivers yawn,
turn toward work. Someone rolls a garbage can
to the curb behind me. A cat slinks along a fence,
stops to twist its neck to check if I am

a threat; I assure it I am not. Perhaps
I remember the high-tide line at the shore,
so my hands curl in my pockets like scotch bonnets.
Some kids await their school bus. Maybe
I am trying to formulate a question or recognize

an answer that anticipates my asking.
A woman holds her phone in one hand,
her dog's leash in the other, while it sniffs out
a suitable place to conduct personal business.
Finished, it barks as I pass. "Shush," she says.

Josh Mahler
WOMAN WITH A SCAR

after Clemens Starck

I walk with hands in my pockets.
It's a cold Sunday morning
and the coat I'm wearing is too thin.
The car tires need cleaning
so I'm heading to the auto store down the road,
certain it's close. I realize I'm wrong
when puffs of breath come more frequently.
No matter. I pay for the good stuff
and return the same way, long shadow
of my body starting to appear.

I keep pace
with the unyielding season,
sunlight parting a pair of clouds.
When will I tame idle thought?
Another item on a list of things to do.

And when I kneel down and use a towel
to wipe away the brake grease,
I think about the woman with the scar.
At work we share an office, talk
everyday, but I never ask how
she got it, sure it's a sensitive story.
And I wouldn't say she's beautiful,
but I wish she was upstairs eating breakfast,
waiting for me to shut the door
and say, "Happy that's done."

I take my time to finish,
checking each tire for spots of grime.
Enough hours remain
after the lock slides into place,
and then there's the silence of the room.

Susannah Sheffer
THE EXTENT TO WHICH

I put my hands right into
the honey, right into the honey
that had spilled onto the plate.
It was messy and unlikely
and not easy to explain
my thinking. How much evidence
does any of us need? I might agree
to step out of my body sometimes.
I might agree to come to you
as an apple or the mountains
or the mud on your shoes.
I might put my hands right into
the mess, right into the mess
we sometimes make together.
I don't think love is obvious at all.
I'm not over the fact of it,
any more than I'm over giraffes
or fermentation or continental drift.
All this will astonish me again
tomorrow, and it should.

Eileen Nittler
HOW TO READ A RIVER

The Willamette River, 187 miles long and north flowing, has its headwaters in the mountains southeast of Eugene in western Oregon. It picks up speed as it flows down the Cascades, tumbling over boulders and downed firs, until it is dammed to form a reservoir. When it finally approaches Eugene, the river is wider and slower—perfect for a kayak float through the city.

My husband and I live one block from the river, and we use it frequently. Over the nearly three decades we've been here, we have kayaked and rafted and canoed in it. We've caught fish, and usually thrown them back. Our dogs retrieved innumerable sticks. Our son and his friends have built rope swings. On hot days, we walk through the shallows and sit in the stream. We move the smooth rocks around to form deeper tubs. Some mornings we bring coffee and sit on the banks to watch for beavers or ducks.

We can read the river when the dams are opened and the flow is faster with snow melt, and when the summer warms and slows it. It is as familiar as our own skin.

The city section of the river does not allow for motorized boats, so this part of the Willamette is used by slower, quieter vessels. We offload our kayaks directly onto the ramp in the city park and push off hard, aiming directly for the far side of the river. This way we can pick up the best current. We glide past an old factory/new apartment building, a sculpture of a heron, a small beach. As we move downstream, we pass under a pedestrian footbridge. I like to think everyone walking above is envious of me, so I'm sure to look as happy as I feel.

Last week though, along with the normal joy of being on the water, I felt an added melancholy, knowing that it was my last time making this journey. After 27 years, we are moving a thousand miles away.

Once, when they were little, the kids caught a crawdad and brought it home to live in the kiddie pool. They named it Skippy. It died within hours, and I still feel badly about it.

Immediately after the foot bridge, we paddle under the car bridge. Cliff swallows nest here in mud-daubed lumps. Why don't they pick the quieter bridge? crosses my mind every time. We stay to the right of the concrete supports. This puts us farther from the branches that stab into the water on the left side and closer to the bike path where graffiti reads "MERCY FORGIVE KINDNESS" in bright colors. It has bothered me for years that those two nouns nestle around a verb.

But this river? We know how to read this river. We are fluent in Willamette.

The sun's warmth balances out the cold of the water when we hit the biggest section of whitewater and get drenched. It's part of the ride to have to bail out. Only once did someone get dumped, and we paddled back upstream to help her get to the shore and back into her boat, albeit missing one shoe.

In the native Kalapuyan language, the river's name is Whilamut, meaning "where the river ripples and runs fast." In English, we explain to visitors, Willamette rhymes with Dammit.

Beyond the rapids, we paddle across to hug the left bank. This is the best place to see the osprey nest. Sometimes there are babies. Every now and then, a bird will swoop down in front of us and carry off a fish in its talons. It's common to see great blue herons—statuesque and patient. On rare occasions, we will see a bald eagle. There is a solo Muscovy duck that lives on the periphery of a flock of geese. That is one ugly bird.

For years, we have walked the bikeway that runs along the banks, picking up litter. We have volunteered to wrap mesh protectors around the trunks of small trees vulnerable to beaver damage. We were told to leave the poison oak, as it is a native—if despised—plant.

Just past the rose garden is where most boaters get stuck. There are two narrow channels you need to look for. Once, we saw an entire bike in the water. We tried to pull it out, but it was stuck on something and wouldn't budge.

Every summer, there is a drowning in the river. We taught the kids to watch for dangerous eddies, to lie on their backs with their feet downstream if they were pulled from shore. They started swimming lessons when they were infants. I still worried about them all the time. How could I not?

Thick blackberry patches, heavy with fruit that perfumes the air, indicate we are near the end of our trip. We make our way back over to the far left and skim along the edge, dodging low-hanging alder branches, moving in and out of shadows which dance on the moving water. These strainers are the biggest hazard on the river. Water can run under without any problems. Not so much with boats or boaters.

Our daughter threw a stick in the river near our house and called her aunt in Portland, 100 miles downstream, to look for it.

There is a river where we're going—the Yellowstone—and I will learn to read it, I know.

Taking out of the water is the hardest part of the trip. If you do it right, you rarely get even one toe wet as you step onto shore. On this final excursion, I was in the water up to my thighs, wrestling with a paddle that wedged itself between a rock and the kayak, while the mighty river tried its hardest to push me over.

As I made it up the bank, the strap on the front of the kayak broke. The boat slid back down the slope, and I was pitched headfirst into a patch of poison oak—one of the patches we weren't supposed to remove.

I turned to look, to say good-bye to my beloved river, a place of both power and pleasure. And then I turned to go home and wash the poison from my skin, and to start the next chapter somewhere new, a chapter I'd learn to read.

Steve Brown
THE BETSIE AT LAKE MICHIGAN

When all else fails,
people settle their prayers
gently into this river.

They come at all hours,
trampling their morning
shadows to the riverbank or else
cutting down autumn panic grass
with nervous, swinging headlights.

Man weeping is a common sight;
woman murmuring alone.
They leave behind an emphatic stillness
foreign to rivers. Emptied, they leave
idle glyphs toed in the sand bar midriver or
drifting in clouds of sienna dust over the parking lot
to express what they cannot.

Most of what they say goes unheard. Most
of what they hear is never spoken aloud.

The supplicants return
home to cities they dislike.
Everyone wishes momentarily
he lived here, nearer water where it is easy
to imagine giving away prayers
and forgetting. Maybe prayers
would not be needed. There is no
stoplight, after all.

Walking the beach sometimes we find prayers
washed up or lolling in breakers near shore:
coming, going; never landing.
Others are smashed in winter storms.
Their pieces we find tangled high in the dune grass
with balloon ribbons and fish spines.

It is taboo to disturb them, to take their power.
And so we are cautious while rummaging
the flayed stomachs of April trout
to see what has sustained them
in secret all winter.

LeAnn Peterson
FOREVER SUMMERTIME

My girl cousins and I crowd around Gramma at the kitchen counter
to watch her cut open a watermelon. Like a warrior, she raises the
curved butcher knife in the air. THWUNK! The knife plunges into the
watermelon, cracking it open into two pieces. Each part is filled with
tight ruby red flesh and tiny flat black seeds. Lifting the knife again and
again, Gramma swiftly cuts the watermelon halves into slices and gives
one to each of us.

   We head out to the front porch and sink our teeth into the cold
grainy sweetness of the watermelon slices on this hot summer night.
Like little bears, we gnaw down into the white rind. Watermelon juice
dribbles down our chins and stains the fronts of our shirts. We sieve the
seeds through our teeth before we spit them out with glee at each other
until the streetlights click on and swarms of mosquitos come out and bite us.

   Gramma calls us to come inside. We're spending the night at her
house. She sends us straight to the bathroom to scrub up with her rose-
scented bar soap at the sink. We brush our teeth, slip our nightgowns
over our heads and go to bed. Sleep will bring us summer dreams of
eating watermelon when we were young.

Ryan Harper
MEADOW: RESIDENT, ALIEN

Could I sit just a while somewhere
I know the glory might trail
the dream. It is a winding yew-
bank ringing me, vagrant —
bounding this way a field, a hay-
maker. In the hedging I see
her tines let fall the grassy
keeps. Fine droops the day-
light and I am raked up,
dried up, as the black and quaking
locust honeys in mayseed.
Away with the rye and fluff
hooping, the tedder, in full pastoral,
unsettles to settle the ruminant,
riffling stoles of feed to the wind,
the ponderous earth. I am the stranger
for the curing. Wakeful to the granger's
work, I would arise and walk
my old stressed beats, easy
with the looser rot — hedging
yew and I and the haymaker
aerate a wish, a way, somewhere.

Michelle DeRose
SHIELDED

I have warmed my paddle-tired, lake-cold
body on exposed Canadian Shield, dark
rock holding radiance past sun-sink,
folding residual heat into the undulance
of my back, buttocks. Damp skin
tingling in grit's scratch and chapped,
breathy kiss. Next morning it offered
its sturdy back to my boots, solid
footing to scoop the day's water.
I pretend it held out all those years for me.

Jim Daniels
LOVE POEM FOR COMMON BRICK WALL,
DETROIT

The scrape of clay and mortar
the mad grizzle of spacing
the maze of a job leading back
to where it started, word

by word, subtle flaws smear
the lines, pauses and restarts
of a life unnoticed, turned
into a numbered address.

Oh, the rough quiet work, row
by row by row, the accumulation
of years, the same puzzle of identical
pieces, incomplete keyboard, mute

music of pride and doubt torn
by the harsh delicacy of dollar bills.
I spread my arms flat and lean in.
I rub my beard against your bricks.

Joshua Zeitler
HISTORIC DOWNTOWN

All these buildings are made of bricks; all these bricks
are tears shed in a local production of Hamlet. Every brick
stands for some ineffable truth. Every brick is lying
down. I used to lie down on the lawn between city hall
and the hardware store when the grass was long, reciting,
To be, or not to be? Now the mayor makes sure it's cut.
He chases loiterers off with a golden rake. I am a kind of rake
in the archaic sense, loose and indiscreet with worms.
I court them with dead deer I find in the road. *One day this
will be me,* I woo, spooning flesh to their lips: *'tis a consummation
devoutly to be wish'd.* I'd like to last a while, but I'm no brick.

Mary Salisbury
FOREVER AND EVER

The mist not moving, a green road bends,
wriggling with frogs. Does life end?
Clouds of chickadees pass overhead,
they drift, then settle in the branches.

I wonder
if the dead want for anything.
The blue sky up ahead, up ahead.

CONTRIBUTOR BIOS

EVE BAINBRIDGE is an after-hours poet whose work has appeared in multiple publications. She has lived around the world and currently resides on the East Coast of the United States.

SHEILA BLACK is the author of five poetry collections and three chapbooks, most recently *For the Loneliness of Walking Out* (Lily Poetry Review Books, 2025). She lives, writes, and hopes for rain in Tempe, AZ, where she is assistant director of the Virginia G. Piper Center for Creative Writing.

***FLEDA BROWN'S** eleventh full-length collection, *The End of the Clockwork Universe*, was published this fall from Carnegie-Mellon University Press. *Doctor of the World* won the 2024 Finishing Line Press Chapbook Contest. Her memoir *Mortality, with Friends* (Wayne State U. P.) is an MIPA Winner and Midwest Book Award winner.

***STEVE BROWN** studied art in Detroit and Germany where his essay collection *Glänze, Gespenst!* was published in 2015. His writing has appeared in *Witness*, *Black Warrior Review*, *DIAGRAM*, and elsewhere. His 2025 poetry collections *Trample & Sew* and *News of Need* can be found at Stevenmatthewbrown.com.

LAUREN CAMP has authored nine books, including *Is Is Enough* (Texas Review Press); and *In Old Sky*, which grew from her experience as Astronomer-in-Residence at Grand Canyon National Park. Honors include a Dorset Prize and Arab American Book Award finalist. She served as New Mexico Poet Laureate. www.laurencamp.com

SHULY XÓCHITL CAWOOD is a writer, teacher, and painter. She is the author of six books, including *Something So Good It Can Never Be Enough* (Press 53) and *Trouble Can Be So Beautiful at the Beginning* (Mercer University Press), winner of the Adrienne Bond Award. Learn more at shulycawood.com.

***JIM DANIELS'** *Late Invocation for Magic: New and Selected Poems* was published by Michigan State University Press in 2026. Other recent books include *An Ignorance of Trees*, nonfiction, and *The Luck of the Fall,* fiction. A native of Detroit, he teaches in the Alma College low-residency MFA program.

IAN DAY is an emerging writer living in Southern California. His work was recently published in *Gold Man Review* and *San Antonio Review.*

***GARY DECOKER,** a retired professor, grew up in Michigan (Detroit and Lexington) and now lives in Glen Arbor and Columbus, Ohio. In addition to his academic research, he enjoys writing personal essays which have appeared in *Allium, Bear Paw, Calendula Review, Kyoto Journal, MacQueen's Quinterly, Minnesota Medicine,* and *Pictura Journal.*

*Professor Emerita of English, **MICHELLE DEROSE** lives with her husband in Grand Rapids, Michigan, where they launch camping, hiking, and canoeing adventures. A Linda Nemec Foster First Book Award finalist, Michelle has published in *The New Verse News, North Coast Voices 2025: Poems of the Great Lakes* (anthology), and *Peninsula Poets*.

CAROLYN FAY is a writer and teacher currently based in Charlottesville, VA. Her short fiction has appeared in literary magazines such as *Orca, BarBar,* and *Paper Dragon*. She holds a Ph.D. in French literature and has a garden that looks like a cemetery.

DIANE GLANCY is a long-time writer. In 2005 she published *The Cubist and the Lost Notebooks of the Painter's Wife. Lazarus, the Intended Writing* is forthcoming in February 2026. Her books are on her website, www.dianeglancy.com. Currently Glancy lives in Texas without a horse or cowboy.

***DAVID B. GUENTHER** was born and raised in Michigan and lives in Ann Arbor. He published his first book, *The Art Dealer's Apprentice* (Rowman & Littlefield), in 2024. His work has also been published in *The Bangalore Review, SAGE Magazine, Tomorrow and Tomorrow,* and other journals.

RYAN HARPER is an Assistant Professor of the Practice at Fairfield University-Bellarmine in Bridgeport, Connecticut. He is the author of *My Beloved Had a Vineyard*, winner of the 2017 Prize Americana in poetry (Poetry Press of Press Americana, 2018). Ryan is the creative arts editor of *American Religion Journal*.

CATHERINE JACOBI earned her MFA in Sculpture from Cranbrook Academy of Art. She is a sculptor whose work explores transformation and value through the use of found materials. Her work is held in several private collections and has been exhibited nationally.

***FELICIA KROL** is a writer and educator based in Detroit, where she works as a Writer-in-Residence with InsideOut Literary Arts and lives alongside many ghosts, her partner, two cats, and one ethereal Dalmatian. Her fiction and poetry have appeared in journals such as *Hayden's Ferry Review, Mid-American Review,* and *Rattle*.

STEFANIE LEE is an ambitious young writer from Montréal, Canada. Living with a rare physical disability called Nemaline Myopathy, she is a motivated software engineering student. When she is not writing or studying, she can be found editing her photography or solving crossword puzzles.

NATHAN LIPPS is the author of *Built Around the Fire* and *the body as passage*. His work can also be found in *Best New Poets, Colorado Review, Cleaver, EcoTheo Review, North American Review, TYPO,* and at nathanlippps.com.

***ELLEN LORD** grew up in the wilds of Northern Michigan. She is a confessional poet with a penchant for humor and melancholy. Her chapbook, *RELATIVE SANITY* (2023) and her poetry book, *VIGIL* (2025), published by Modern History Press, are available wherever new books are sold. ellenlordauthor.com.

JOSH MAHLER lives and writes in Virginia. His poems have appeared in *Denver Quarterly, Tar River Poetry, Quarter After Eight, South Dakota Review, The Louisville Review, The Carolina Quarterly, Valparaiso Poetry Review, Potomac Review, The Southern Poetry Anthology,* from Texas Review Press, and elsewhere.

***KATHLEEN MCGOOKEY** has published five books and four chapbooks, most recently *Cloud Reports* (Celery City Chapbooks) and *Paper Sky* (Press 53). Her work has appeared in many journals including *Copper Nickel, Epoch, Glassworks, Hunger Mountain, Los Angeles Review, North American Review,* and *The Southern Review.* She lives in Middleville, Michigan.

***KAT MOORE** has prose in *Craft Literary, Brevity, River Teeth (Beautiful Things), Diagram, Image,* and others. She was a 2021 Bread Loaf Writers Conference Scholar. She is currently the recipient of a Post-Doctoral Fellowship in Creative Writing at Central Michigan University where she teaches creative writing and literature.

***CAMILLE NEWSOM** is the author of the chapbook *This Suffering and Scrumptious World* (Galileo Press, 2023) and *Purgatory Junkie* (Main Street Rag, 2025). Based in West Michigan, Camille is an educator and land steward. Her poems have appeared in *ONE ART, Terrain.org,* and *Southword,* among others.

EILEEN NITTLER lives in Montana now, which is shockingly different but exciting as well. She writes, explores, and looks for beauty in the world around her (and sometimes finding it). She has previously been published in *Oregon Humanities, The Chicago Story Press,* and *Pacific Review,* among others.

basil payne (they/them) is a queer poet-artist who can be found in Logan, Utah's trees. Their work can be found in *Sugar House Review, Sheepshead Review, Oyster River Pages,* and occasionally Utah State University's Projects Gallery.

***LEANN PETERSON** lives in Grand Rapids, MI. She enjoys writing about people, places, and things that are close to her heart. LeAnn's work has been published in *Michigana, The Detroit Free Press,* and *Dunes Review.*

***CHRISTINE RHEIN** is the author of *Wild Flight* (Walt McDonald Book Prize, Texas Tech University Press). Her poems have appeared in *The Southern Review, Michigan Quarterly Review,* and *Rattle,* and in many anthologies, including *The Best American Nonrequired Reading.* A former automotive engineer, Christine lives in Brighton, Michigan.

MORGAN ROSE-MARIE is a queer writer and an Assistant Professor at Utah Valley University. She has a PhD from Ohio University and an MA from Colorado State University. Her work has been featured in *The Normal School, Heavy Feather Review, Tampa Review,* and *Pleiades,* among others.

MARY SALISBURY'S poetry has been published in *Michigan Quarterly Review, North Dakota Review,* and other journals. She is the author of two poetry chapbooks (Finishing Line Press) and a short-story collection (Main Street Rag). An Oregon Literary Arts Fellowship recipient, Mary earned her MFA in writing from Pacific University.

SUSANNAH SHEFFER'S newest poetry collection, *The Stone Tries to Understand the Hands,* was published by Cornerstone Press in 2025. Her previous collections include *Break and Enter* (2021) and *This Kind of Knowing* (2013). She lives in Western Massachusetts.

ELLA SHIVELY is a writer and naturalist from Wisconsin. She is currently working toward her MFA in Poetry at Cornell University. Her writing has been published in *RockPaperPoem, Poetose, Dipity, SoFloPoJo,* and elsewhere. You can find her on Instagram @shivelywrites.

***MOLLIE THOMAS** is a writer living in Traverse City, Michigan with her husband, two kids, and one very misbehaved dog. She received her Master of Arts from Emerson College in Writing, Literature and Publishing. "Even Flowers" is her first published piece of fiction.

ERIC WEIL lives in Raleigh, NC. His poems have appeared recently, or are forthcoming, in *Kakalak 2025, Had I a Dove* (an anthology of poems about the Hurricane Helene destruction in Appalachia), *Brillig, River and South Review,* and *North Coast Voices.* He has three chapbooks in print.

***CASEY JO GRAHAM WELMERS** holds a BA in English, Language and Literature from The University of Michigan and practices written and healing arts from the Great Lakes state. Find her most recent work in *Bending Genres, Stanchion, Pangyrus* and more, and at caseyjo.carrd.co.

***JAN WORTH** is a poet and essayist whose new chapbook, *Elegies from the Last Days of the Empire,* is forthcoming from Kelsay Books. A longtime resident of Flint, Michigan, she cherishes her old house on a tree-lined street where she cares for her husband and follows the lives of birds.

***GLEN YOUNG** is co-editor of Walloon Writers Review and co-director of Top of the Mitt Writing Project. He is a ski instructor and a kayak guide. He also teaches creative writing, dividing time between Petoskey and Mackinac Island with his wife Jane Benjamin Young.

***JOSHUA ZEITLER** is a queer, nonbinary writer based in rural Michigan. They are the author of the chapbook *Bliss Road* (Seven Kitchens Press, 2025), and their work has appeared in *Ploughshares, Foglifter, Anacapa Review, Wildness,* and elsewhere.

* denotes Michigan native or resident

STAFF BIOS

*KELLI FITZPATRICK is an author, editor, and teacher from Michigan. Her first novel, *Captain Marvel: Carol Danvers Declassified*, is available from BenBella Books. Her short fiction has been published by Simon and Schuster, Baen Books, Flash Fiction Online, and others. She holds an MFA in Creative Writing from Iowa State University. Website: KelliFitzpatrick.com

*CHRIS GIROUX received his doctorate from Wayne State University and is a professor of English at Saginaw Valley State University, where he has served as faculty advisor for the school's literary magazine and co-founded the community arts journal *Still Life*. His second chapbook, *Sheltered in Place*, was released in 2022.

*STEFEN HOLTREY is a poet and speculative fiction writer from Traverse City, Michigan. His work has appeared in *Dunes Review*, *The Raw Art Review*, and *The Cosmic Background*. He was a member of the 2018 Futurescapes Writers' Workshop and is a graduate of the 2022 Clarion Writers' Workshop. He lives with a cat, four chickens, and a wonderful wife.

*ANNE-MARIE OOMEN is Michigan Author for 2023-24. Her memoir, *As Long As I Know You: The Mom Book* won AWP's Sue William Silverman Nonfiction Award. She wrote *Lake Michigan Mermaid* with Linda Nemec Foster, *Love, Sex and 4-H* (Next Generation Indie Award/Memoir), and others. *The Lake Huron Mermaid* is most recent, now out.

*JOHN MAUK has published a range of stories and nonfiction works, including his full collections, *Field Notes for the Earthbound* and *Where All Things Flatten*. John also hosts Prose from the Underground, a YouTube video series for working writers. For more information, see johnmauk.com.

*SARA MAURER lives with her family in Michigan's Upper Peninsula. She honed her creative writing craft while completing Stanford's Continuing Studies Novel Writing Certificate program. Her debut novel, *A Good Animal*, is coming February 24, 2026 from St. Martin's Press. Find her at www.saramaurerwrites.com.

*TERESA SCOLLON's fourth poetry collection, *No Trouble Staying Awake*, is now out from Cornerstone Press. A National Endowment for the Arts fellow, she teaches the Writers Studio program at North Ed Career Tech in Traverse City.

*YVONNE STEPHENS is a poet, rural librarian, amateur mycologist and mental health activist. *The Salt Before It Shakes* was published by Hidden Timber Books in 2017. Her work has appeared in *Dunes Review*, *Family Stories from the Attic*, *Eucalypt*, and *iō Literary Journal*.

*JENNIFER YEATTS' literary life has included MA and MFA degrees in poetry, teaching writing in various forms, a handful of small publications, and editorial roles at *Passages North* and *Fugue*. For money, she teaches people about coffee and Pilates.

LOOK WHO'S BEEN HERE...

Carl Hiaasen, David Sedaris, Margaret Atwood, Jason Reynolds, Alice Walker, Tom Brokaw, Pete Souza, Ann Patchett, Amy Tan, Fredrik Backman, Jeannette Walls, Mitch Albom, Diane Rehm

YOU WON'T BELIEVE WHO'S COMING NEXT!

The National Writers Series of Traverse City is a nonprofit organization dedicated to holding great conversations with today's best authors and building the creative writing skills of youth.

For information on author events, student writing classes, Battle of the Books, college scholarships and more, visit

NationalWritersSeries.com

SUBMISSION GUIDELINES

Dunes Review welcomes work from writers at all stages of their careers living anywhere in the world, though we particularly love featuring those with ties to Michigan and the Midwest. We are open to all styles and aesthetics, but please read the following carefully to dive a little deeper into what we're looking for.

Ultimately, we're looking for work that draws us in from the very first line: with image, with sound, with sense, with lack of sense. We're looking for writing that makes us *feel* and bowls us over, lifts us up, and takes us places we've never been to show us ordinary things in ways we've never seen them. We're looking for poems and stories and essays that teach us how to read them and pull us back to their beginnings as soon as we've read their final lines. We're looking for things we can't wait to read again, things we can't resist sharing with the nearest person who will listen. Send us your best work. We'll give it our best attention.

Submissions are accepted only via our Submittable platform: www.dunesreview.submittable.com. We do not consider work sent through postal mail or email. Any submissions sent through email will not be read or responded to. Please see further guidelines posted on our site. We look forward to reading your work!

Join our community of Michigan Writers!

Annual membership: $50 / Student rate: $20

Membership includes:

• Our monthly email newsletter to stay up to date with events;

• Two annual issues of *Dunes Review*, Northern Michigan's premier literary journal;

• Free admission to Michigan Writers workshops;

• Eligibility for the annual Michigan Writers Cooperative Press chapbook contest;

• And ... well, since we're an organization of members, you decide!

To become a member, visit www.michwriters.org/join

Call for Patrons

What you're reading is pretty special, because the *Dunes Review:*

• Has been continuously published for 28 years
• Is the work of an all-volunteer organization (rather than an educational institution)
• Is still available in print
• Helps newer writers get into print alongside established writers

The cost of publication can be underwritten in part by individual contributions. We invite you to support the publication of the next issue with a donation of $50. Send your check payable to **Michigan Writers** to:

Michigan Writers, P.O. Box 2355

Traverse City, MI 49685

Thank you for your support!

Questions? Contact us at info@michwriters.org.

www.ingramcontent.com/pod-product-compliance
Lightning Source LLC
Chambersburg PA
CBHW021741190726
48288CB00009B/3131